EMILE VERHAEREN
POEMS

Emile Verhaeren
POEMS

Selected, translated
& introduced by
WILL STONE

With a Preface by
PATRICK McGUINNESS

Arc
PUBLICATIONS
2014

Published by Arc Publications,
Nanholme Mill, Shaw Wood Road
Todmorden OL14 6DA, UK
www.arcpublications.co.uk

Design by Tony Ward
Printed in Great Britain by
TJ International, Padstow, Cornwall

978 1904614 69 2 (pbk)
978 1906570 09 5 (hbk)

Cover photo: Verhaeren standing at the window
of his cottage at Caillou-qui-bique, 1914,
photo by Charles Bernier.

Arc Publications and the translator wish to express special thanks to
the Ministère de la Communauté française and the Académie Royal de
langue et de la littérature françaises in Brussels for their generous support and patience in the realization of this project.

**'Arc Classics' Translation Series –
New Translations of Great Poets of the Past
Series Editor: Jean Boase-Beier**

TRANSLATOR'S ACKNOWLEDGEMENTS

This collection of translations sifted from the prodigious poetic archive of Emile Verhaeren was the result of considerable labour over a prolonged period of time. It demanded the focus and energies not only of myself, but of others whose contribution must here be recognised. My first port of call however is with the various organisations who recognised the case for support towards the realisation of this collection, the first to be published in English since the immediate aftermath of the poet's death in 1916.

Firstly my gratitude goes to The Society of Authors in London and Arts Council England (East). Their assistance enabled me to carry out extended research into Verhaeren's life and to procure illustrative materials for the book. In France I was further assisted by the Centre National du Livre (CNL) in Paris. I also had the good fortune to spend a residence at the Centre International des Traducteurs Littéraires (CITL) in Arles to work on the project. Special thanks however must go to their Belgian counterpart, the Collège Européen des Traducteurs Littéraires de Seneffe, and to its president Jacques de Decker and director Françoise Wuilmart, whose faith, generosity and continued hospitality down the years have allowed me to accomplish the task of translation over a number of residences. I should also like to thank Mr Paul Etienne Kisters in the Archives et Musée de la Littérature for his time and trouble in tracking down certain photographs and for enabling me to view Verhaeren's possessions and personal library, and the courteous staff of the Cabinet des Estampes in the Bibliothèque Royal de Belgique for their expert guidance in the procurement of prints. I am grateful too for the assistance given by Jean Luc Outers, head of the Ministère de la Communauté française department 'Promotion des Lettres', and also Entrez-Lire and the Passa Porta international bookshop in Brussels.

A number of individuals also earned my gratitude either for their advice on the texts, with aspects of Verhaeren's biography, or simply for their sincere support and belief in the importance of bringing Verhaeren's poetry out of the shadows. They are the following: distinguished scholar of Belgian symbolism, Professor Michel Otten in Brussels, Verhaeren biographer Dr. Beatrice Worthing in England and Dr. Rik Hemmerijckx, inspirational curator of the Museum Emile Verhaeren in Sint Amands. A number of other individuals must also be thanked for their instinctive rallying around the English Verhaeren. They are Marie-Pierre Devroedt in Brussels for her unselfish assistance and advice on the texts; Michaël Vanderbril and Sven Peeters in Antwerp for their friendship and devotion to the promotion of Belgian literature abroad; Anette Van de Wiele in Bruges for her warm support and tracking down of elusive texts; Professor Emeritus Clive Scott, University of East Anglia, for his perennial belief in the project; Stephen Romer for his fraternal counsel and fin-de-siècle empathies; Paul Stubbs for his enthusiasm and awareness of Verhaeren's importance in the European canon; and lastly book designer Emma Mountcastle in Devon for her necessary conversion to Verhaerenism and daily administerings of the contents of the original manuscript of Beatrice Worthing's highly accomplished English biography of the poet. Finally, I should like to thank the *Black Herald* literary magazine in Paris and *The Wolf* poetry magazine in England for publishing a number of these Verhaeren translations in advance of the book.

CONTENTS

Preface / 9
Introduction / 11
A Note on the Texts / 30

LIST OF ILLUSTRATIONS

Period photographs by courtesy of the Archive et Musée de la Littérature, Bruxelles and the Museum Emile Verhaeren, Sint Amands.

"Everything in our culture is contrast: we treasure the opposi-
tions that coexist inside us." Thus Emile Verhaeren in the 1890s,
optimistically defining the extraordinary flowering of art, literature
and architecture in *fin de siècle* Belgium. For all his originality,
Emile Verhaeren was the product of his place and time: a country barely fifty years old in which the mix of Germanic Flemish
and Latinate French created a generation of writers and artists of
international significance. Verhaeren, along with his contemporaries Maurice Maeterlinck, Georges Rodenbach, Albert Mockel,
Charles van Lerberghe and Max Elskamp, helped to define the
Symbolist movement.

We talk of 'French' Symbolism, and we are right, but only inso-
far as it happened in (and to) the French language. Symbolism was
the first consciously 'francophone' literary movement, drawing to
Paris and Brussels writers from places as diverse as Poland, Canada,
the USA, Switzerland, Russia and Latin America. What they all
had in common was a sense of what Mallarmé called "le double
état de la parole" – "the double state of the word". It's a gnomic
statement, but Mallarmé expands a little: "brut ou immediate ici,
là essentiel" – "raw or immediate here; there essential". For the
Belgians, everything was in a double state – Belgium itself was a
'double state' – and Verhaeren and his contemporaries understood
that what made them the perfect writers to define Symbolism as
both a movement and an approach to poetic language was this
consciousness of their own cultural duality.

Like Rodenbach and Maeterlinck, Verhaeren wrote in French,
but allowed his Flemish heritage to infiltrate and infuse his
poetry. We might say that he used Flemish to de-Latinize his
French, which is colourful, rough, often unbridled and *houleux*,
stormy. His poetry works at a mythical and symbolic level, shot
through with surprising imagery and extended metaphors, but he
is always true to the social realities of his time. Collections such
as *Les Villes tentaculaires* and *Les Campagnes hallucinées* evoke, in
dream-like, sometimes nightmarish, language the radical social
and demographic changes of modernity: industrialization, rural
depopulation, land-and city-scapes transformed for ever by work
but also worklessness, by money, technology, mechanization and
the machine-age. This explains in part why he remained such a

popular poet among the Socialists and Communists of the twentieth century long after his more rarefied, solipsistic contemporaries had been forgotten.

Verhaeren is always a lyric poet, whether describing the architectural treasures of Flemish *béguinages* or the broken factory windows of an unnamed industrial city. He is proud of the rich impurity of his language, which is a world and a culture away from the transparent classical rationality of French. Verhaeren's French is dynamic, instinctive, exclamatory, close to the intimate voice yet also vatic and prophetic. Unlike so many of his Symbolist contemporaries, he is unafraid of the future, and it is no surprise that when the Futurists drew up their list of admired predecessors, Verhaeren is chief among them. But he was also a poet of the inner landscape, of the heart and mind, of suffering and isolation and self-torture. Verhaeren was by nature an optimist, especially in his last few books, but even his pessimism is alive and variegated, full of energy and vigour. In 'The Crown' he writes "Yes, I too would like my crown of thorns / and one for every thought, red hot, across / my brow, right into my brain, to the frail roots / where sins and forged dreams writhe / within me, through me". Verhaeren, like Baudelaire, is adept at finding concrete ways of expressing abstract or numinous feelings; and like Baudelaire, he is especially fond of the jarring but memorable simile, the forcible yoking together, with a kind of tender violence, of like and the unlike into an image. We may see the continuation of his voice and vision not just in the work of the Futurists but also in the Expressionist poetry of Germany, where his work was read and admired well into the twentieth century, and into the work of the Surrealists, who learned from his audacious image-making how to satisfy the dual-pull of expressing the inner and the outer worlds.

Verhaeren seems to us, nearly a hundred years after his death, uniquely modern, yet at the same time carrying with him something unreconstructedly romantic: a sense of the poet as visionary, a belief that the poet can include the world and not simply refine it away or stun it with words, and that poetry itself has the appetite not just to observe Progress but to be part of it. These translations stay true to his spirit but also to the *élan* of his Flemish-inflected French, and carry him across into English admirably.

Patrick McGuinness

INTRODUCTION

"With his own breath Verhaeren enlarged the horizon of the little motherland, and like Balzac with his thankless mild Touraine, he grafted onto the Flemish plains the beautiful human kingdom of his ideality and his art."

FRANCIS VIELÉ-GRIFFIN[1]

"Of Verhaeren one might say that he met this surprising challenge of 'incarnating a country which did not exist', of granting it a soul, a great soul, and making it coincide with the universal soul. Emerging from a debilitating terrain, he managed by an extraordinary effort of comprehension and assimilation to become the poet of his century and the mirror of European civilisation."

JACQUES MARX[2]

"A dark day, I still remember clearly and will never forget. I took out his letters, his many letters, all of them laid out in front of me, so as to read them, be alone with them, to bring to a close that which was over now, for I knew I would never receive another. And yet I could not. There was something within that prevented me from saying farewell to him who resided in me as proof incarnate of my own existence, of my faith on earth. The more I told myself he was dead, the more I felt how much he lived and breathed in me still and even these words which I am writing to take leave of him have merely revived him. For only the admission of a great loss attests to the true possession of that which must perish and only the unforgettable dead are fully alive in our midst!"

STEFAN ZWEIG[3]

"My heart is a burning bush that sets my lips on fire...": this expressively visionary line from a poem by Émile Verhaeren, Belgium's most celebrated and significant poet of the modern age, serves not only to signal an exceptional lyrical gift, but also reveals the strain of his fiery Flemish nature. Born and educated in Flanders but, like his contemporaries, drawn to write in French, the language favoured by the cultured middle classes and intellectual circles of the period, Verhaeren produced a body of work that encompasses the period of Symbolism of the late 1880s and 1890s and also witnesses the first tentative steps of

11

Modernism in a new century. It was this new century and its unprecedented social, technological and scientific eruptions that Verhaeren, more than any other poet of his generation, sought to express in the most truthful lyrical fashion. Although remembered mainly as a poet, Verhaeren was also a prolific playwright and a shrewd art critic. Beyond this he was nothing less than a monumental presence on the stage of Franco-Belgian literature for a quarter of a century, his name at the heart of almost all significant developments in the literary and artistic communities of Brussels and Paris.

Verhaeren was an inveterate traveller and made countless extended journeys into Europe. Spain, Germany and France were his favoured destinations, although it was the teeming metropolis of London that particularly seized his imagination early on and later served as the principal cityscape for *Les Villes tentaculaires* [The Tentacular Towns], his landmark collection of 1895. In the years preceding the First World War, Verhaeren's fame as a poet and a speaker snowballed and by the time of his death in 1916, he was translated into twenty languages, his name known not only across Europe but as far as Russia and South America. Verhaeren regularly filled lecture halls in the major cities of Europe, and in Germany, where his profile was enhanced by the strenuous efforts of his dedicated disciple, the Austrian writer Stefan Zweig, the sales of his poetry were considerable. Fêted by both the Belgian and English royal families, he enjoyed a certain celebrity during the early years of the war as spiritual envoy for a beleaguered Belgium. It was after delivering a speech to the exiled Belgian community in Rouen, in November 1916, that Verhaeren met his death, accidentally falling beneath the train that was to take him back to his home in Paris.

I

Emile Verhaeren was born on 21 May 1855 (the same year as his fellow poet Georges Rodenbach) in the village of Sint Amands situated on a deep bend of the River Scheldt as it winds its way towards Antwerp. These days, Sint Amands is known chiefly as the poet's resting place – the solemn and imposing black marble tomb containing his and his wife Marthe's remains holds a prominent place on the river bank – but Verhaeren's

12

memories of the village and surrounding countryside are vividly present in a number of the poems in this collection. Although he wrote his literary works in French, Verhaeren's pride in his native Flanders and a sensitivity for its guileless, voluptuous and earthy character, infuse his work.

From 1868 to 1874, Verhaeren attended the noted College Sainte Barbe in Ghent where he became close friends with Georges Rodenbach, later to be the celebrated poet and prose painter of Bruges. Maurice Maeterlinck would also attend this college and go on to pip Verhaeren to the post by winning the Nobel Prize in 1912. Verhaeren was enrolled as a law student from 1875-1881 at the Catholic University of Louvain and although called to the bar, he turned his back on law and became prominent in an avant garde literary movement around a new magazine called *La Jeune Belgique*, founded in 1881 by the poet Max Waller. The poets and artists who published there declaimed a radical new society which with uncompromising zeal always put creativity first; "art for art's sake" was its clarion call. Their heroes included Baudelaire, Gautier, Leconte de Lisle, Banville, Daudet and Flaubert. In the same year another review, *L'Art moderne*, which was largely concerned with criticism, appeared. Along with playwright and journalist Edmond Picard and writer and critic Octave Maus, Verhaeren was instrumental in its inception and in that of the artist movement known as 'Les XX' associated with it. Formed in 1883, 'Les XX' was a collective of twenty Belgian painters, sculptors and designers who held an annual exhibition of their art in Brussels to which the leading artists of the day were invited from Paris. Monet, Gauguin, Seurat, Cézanne and Van Gogh all made one or more visits to the Brussels exhibitions and Verhaeren formed lasting friendships with Seurat, Signac and others. In this period, Verhaeren also met the now elderly poet Paul Verlaine whose authenticity as a poet, lack of adherence to any school or trend, and odd mixture of vulnerability and pathological resilience set against an almost sacred naivety, deeply impressed Verhaeren.

Once ensconced in Brussels and with his writing career underway, Verhaeren wrote prolifically. His reviews, prefaces, essays and articles were widely published in leading journals and periodicals and his fame grew through manifold translations. But it was in *L'Art moderne* that he cemented his reputation as an art critic. His brilliant essay of 1908 on the artist James Ensor is still highly regarded today and one can find his name associated with key writings on Rembrandt, Rubens, Khnopff, Van Rysselberghe, Redon, Moreau, Brangwyn, Millet and many more. He was well received too by Rodin in Paris; a friendship blossomed and in 1915 the great sculptor candidly presented the poet with the plaster of an upturned face entitled 'La Douleur' [Pain]. In their turn, the artists reciprocated by copiously illustrating his works or providing frontispieces for his first editions; the collection *Les Soirs* [The Evenings, 1888] for example, carried both a frontispiece by Redon and ornamentation by Khnopff. Later works were illustrated by the reclusive Léon Spilliaert (1881-1946), whose unsettling symbolism and morbidly-imbued visions were in accord with the tenor of Verhaeren's work. But it was the Old Masters who really shifted the foundations of Verhaeren's imagination: Flemish Primitive painters, of course, and Rubens in Flanders, Rembrandt in Holland, Velasquez and Goya in Spain. Towering above all, however, was one Matthias Grünewald whose 'Isenheim Altarpiece' in Colmar, with its crucified, putrefying Christ twisted in agony at the command of a rough wooden cross, bored into the poet with an almost hallucinatory intensity of expressive possibility. For Verhaeren, Grünewald was the ultimate painterly synthesis of his own mental suffering and violently restless imagination.

Although the factions of *L'Art moderne* and *La Jeune Belgique* competed for years for the soul of Belgian literature, as the manifestation of Symbolism intensified through the mid-eighties, it was a new magazine created by critic and poet Albert Mockel, *La Wallonie*, that became the unrivalled voice of the Symbolist movement in Belgium. From its appearance around 1886, the Symbolist poets of France and Belgium consolidated their union, with the poet Stephane Mallarmé as their figurehead. Around the axle of his famously enriching Salons – or 'mardis' as they came to be known as they occurred on a Tuesday – the individual bearings of Symbolism moved, enhancing revolution.

Verhaeren made frequent trips to Paris, quickly befriending Mallarmé, and finally moved there – after nearly two decades at the heart of the Brussels literary community – in 1898, ironically the same year in which both Rodenbach and Mallarmé died. He remained there until 1916, living modestly in a worker's house in St. Cloud with his wife Marthe Massin, a watercolourist, whom he married in 1891.

In the years leading up to the First World War, Verhaeren's presence on the European stage progressed to the point at which he became a natural torchbearer for an ideal of cultural fraternity in Europe, a resurgence of dignified artistic endeavour with a social conscience. This optimism (with socialist utopian trappings) was most clearly defined in his middle to late period work, particularly *Les Forces tumultueuses* [The Tumultuous Forces, 1902] and led to his being dubbed 'the Belgian Walt Whitman', a tag that remains to this day, but which is only partially appropriate in that Verhaeren's work was much more raw, overwhelmingly expressive and 'hallucinated' than Whitman's.

On the threshold of his fifties, and firmly established as a significant European poet and thinker, Verhaeren was routinely acclaimed with each new publication and was in great demand across the continent as a speaker. According to Stefan Zweig, however, he was unconcerned about money or glory, his passion for articulating life with uncompromising truthfulness being paramount and commanding all his energies. In the *pointilliste* painting 'The Reading of Verhaeren' (1903) by lifelong friend Théo Van Rysellberghe, we see the poet in a flame-coloured jacket with hand demonstratively raised, holding forth to a room of soberly attentive and perhaps somewhat intimidated fellow writers among whom can be identified Maeterlinck, Gide and Francis Vielé-Griffin.

Verhaeren's reach had by now extended to the United Kingdom where a number of respected writers and critics, among them Edmund Gosse and Arthur Symons, had championed his work through the nineties. An English translation by Jethro Bithell of Stefan Zweig's reverential biography, *Emile Verhaeren* (1910), appeared with Constable in 1914. Aldous Huxley wrote a witty and insightful essay on Verhaeren in his collection *On the Margin* (1923) followed, in 1926, by the rather academic and now somewhat dated study (*Verhaeren: a Study in the Development of His Art and Ideas*) by Percy Mansell Jones. In the 1950s

an English scholar named
Beatrice Worthing produced
a highly-informed, in-depth
biography of Verhaeren which,
never having found a publisher
in the UK, only received the
recognition it deserved when it
was translated into French and
finally published, to considerable acclaim, by Verhaeren's old
French publisher Le Mercure
de France in 1992. More recently, a comprehensive modern biography, *Verhaeren: biographie d'une œuvre* by Jacques
Marx appeared in Belgium in
1996. In late 2012, *Emile Ver-*

haeren, Vlaamse dichter voor Europa, a new biography in Dutch
by Paul Servaes, ex-curator of the Verhaeren Museum in Sint
Amands, was published and launched at the Museum. The most
influential figure for Verhaeren's reputation in England during
his lifetime was the critic and translator Edward Osmans, who
invited the poet to England on several occasions to stay with him
and his family, using his influence and contacts to further his
name. But despite their interest and the passionate admiration
of certain individuals, the English struggled to assess Verhaeren
conclusively, seeing him first as a Zola-inspired realist, then as
a 'decadent' poet of the nineties, then as the wild progeny of
Victor Hugo and Whitman.

Russia, on the other hand, gearing up for revolution, was
poised to applaud Verhaeren's achievements. From around
1906, with the support of the poet Brioussov, he was widely
published in reviews; his urgent spiritual manifestos seemed to
strike a particular chord with the Russians as they had previ-
ously with the Germans. Even the great poet Alexander Blok
attempted to translate him and Anna Akhmatova evokes his
name in her memories of Blok. And in 1916, when Verhaeren
died, Mayakovsky alluded to the cruelty of his sudden absence
in his collection *Darkness*:

One after another the greats pass on
    colossus after colossus…
        today above Verhaeren the skies are furious.

Closer to home, André Gide wrote that Verhaeren was the most accomplished poet writing in French at the turn of the century, declaiming: "You are our only epic poet and I hold you in an esteem above all others." For the poet Rainer Maria Rilke, Verhaeren was a senior figure, a master in the same vein as Rodin, a living example of artistic integrity and uncompromising creative labour. Since arriving in Paris in 1902, Rilke had made the French capital the necessary anchorage between his disparate European sojourns and was to become as regular a visitor at St. Cloud as he was at Meudon. Rilke's respect and admiration for Verhaeren was like that of Stefan Zweig, profound and long-lasting. The scrupulously respectful messages and dedications he left in books given to the older poet, struggle to express the devotion he felt: "To my dear and great Verhaeren, your Rilke. St. Cloud 11th January, 1909" or, as he wrote, simply, in a copy of the *Cornet*, "For Emile Verhaeren, intensely… Rilke". When he was completing his famous *Elegies* and *Sonnets to Orpheus*, Rilke wrote a short prose text, *Letter of a Young Worker,* addressed to a mysterious 'Monsieur V' whose identity was, in fact, Verhaeren. Following the First World War and Verhaeren's death, Rilke read his later collections avidly and in his letters is seen to recommend them to a number of friends. In *La Multiple splendeur* [The Multiple Splendour, 1906], *Les Forces tumultueuses* and, perhaps most pertinently, in the posthumous collection *Les Flammes hautes* [The High Flames, 1917], Rilke found an inflexible will and energy in truth-seeking that seemed in alignment with the approach to poetry which he himself had so patiently been edging towards. And although Verhaeren was evidently a very different poet to the more mysterious and introspective Rilke, his world-affirming objectivity and unquenchable life force served to energize his perennially self-questioning friend.

It was Stefan Zweig who took it upon himself to forge Verhaeren's reputation in Germany and the correspondence between the two men shows the inexhaustible energy expended in the fulfilment of this task. Zweig felt Verhaeren's poetic impulse keenly and recognised the sacrifice of those interminable stretches of solitude in hostile environments that gave rise to great poems.

He describes in his memoirs, for example, how Verhaeren would travel around London: "Often he remained for hours on the top deck of an omnibus better to see the throng, eyes closed better to feel this muffled drone penetrate into him, like the rustling of a forest…". Zweig would often visit the Verhaerens in Paris or, for five consecutive summers, joined them in Caillou-qui-bique in southern Belgium close to the French border where Verhaeren retreated to his remote country cottage during the seasonal break to experience the simplicity of a rural idyll as yet untouched by modernity. (It was the countryside around Caillou which informed much of Verhaeren's later work and crucially the series of love poems he dedicated to Marthe.) The two men unknowingly parted for the last time in the unsettling summer of 1914 when, as a European war loomed, Zweig was obliged to leave Belgium abruptly on the last Orient Express bound for Germany:

> It was in the spring, that terrible spring of 1914. The horrendous year had begun. Quite gently, peacefully it advanced and ripened into the summer. We were due to meet. I would spend the month of August with Verhaeren, but I had already been in Belgium since July to spend three weeks by the sea. En route, I stopped off for a day in Brussels and my first priority as soon as I arrived was to go and see Verhaeren at his friend Montald's house. A tram took me along a wide avenue, then through open fields, leading me to Woluwe where I duly found Verhaeren with Montald, who had just finished his portrait, the last one to be made! What joy to see him there! We spoke of his last works, of his 'Flammes hautes', whose last verses he read aloud to me, of his drama 'Les Aubes', which he was revising for Reinhardt; we spoke of friends and of the summer which would bring us fresh joys and new pleasures. We only bade a brief farewell, since we would be seeing each other soon in his country cottage. To say goodbye, he clasped me in his arms. I should arrive on 2nd August and he shouted after me one more time: the 2nd, the 2nd of August! Alas, little did we know the significance of the date we had so casually arranged in that moment. The tram crossed fields bathed with summer. I watched him for a long time, waving to me by Montald's side, until I could see nothing more…[4]

With the outbreak of war in the late summer of 1914, the dream of a cultural European union pursued so ardently by

Verhaeren, Zweig, Rolland and their circle was brutally swept aside by the pandemic of nationalist fervour and politically orchestrated hatred between foes. The wilful destruction of ancient towns such as Louvain, of priceless libraries and works of art and the slaughter of innocents by German forces on Belgian soil had a devastating effect on the acutely sensitive Verhaeren. For him, all relations with Germany, literary or otherwise, were now at an end. Faced with atrocities on such a scale, he allowed himself, in spite of his anti-nationalist convictions, to be infected by hatred for the foe and began to write vitriolic texts against Germany – ironically the country that before this outbreak of barbarism had seen the greatest support for his poetry – and German culture. The switch was extreme, for even as war fever grew in the late summer of 1914, Zweig, Rilke and their Insel publisher, Kippenberg, had met in a restaurant in Paris to flesh out the plan for a Collected Works of Verhaeren in German and were already in the process of farming out the works to various translators (Zweig himself was apparently to tackle *La Multiple splendeur*). Then war broke out and the project was abandoned, never to be resumed. Zweig, trapped behind impassable frontiers, asked for news of Verhaeren. But the line of communication had gone dead. Verhaeren's fury at Germany's scorched earth policy in Belgium took the form of a book called *La Belqique sanglante* [Belgium Bleeding], a visceral anti-German polemic quickly translated into English and published first in *The Observer* in 1914, then in book form in 1915. Even in a letter thanking his Russian hosts after a conference in Moscow in 1915, Verhaeren took the opportunity of warmly praising Russian culture while denouncing its German counterpart. A collection of poetry expressing similarly anti-teutonic sentiments, *Les Ailes rouges de la guerre* [The Red Wings of War], was published in 1916 but by then Verhaeren's unbridled animosity was giving way to a more rationally balanced position, and that same year he began to send out feelers to old friends across the frontier, full of contrition for his earlier blind support of this 'lamentable division of nations'.

This tentative drawing back of the Germanic satellites into his orbit was rudely terminated by Verhaeren's death in Rouen and Zweig was never to see the reunion he so craved. His reverence for Verhaeren never faltered and with his untimely death, took on an almost messianic property. In *Errinerungen an Emile Verhaeren* [Memories of Emile Verhaeren], published in Vienna in 1917, he recalled the emotion of their early encounter and revealed the essence of Verhaeren's beguiling character:

> For the first time I felt the grasp of his vigorous hand, for the first time met his clear kindly glance. He arrived as he always did brimming over with enthusiasm and the experiences of the day. As he fell to his meal he began to talk…With the first word he went straight to the essence of people, because he was himself completely open, open to everything new, rejecting nothing, ready for every individual… it seemed as if he projected his whole being towards you. He knew as yet nothing of me, but was already full of gratitude for my inclination, already he offered me his trust simply because he heard I was close to his work. And in spite of myself, all shyness faded before the stormy onslaught of his being. I felt myself free, as never before, in the face of this unknown, open man. His gaze, strong, steely and clear, unlocked my heart.

It was on 27 November 1916 that a weary Verhaeren, having given a rousing speech to appreciative Belgian exiles in Rouen, fell beneath the train for Paris in an attempt to board it prematurely to secure a seat. Fatally injured, he died shortly afterwards on the platform, reportedly (though falsely, it is now claimed) uttering the words: "Je meurs, ma femme, ma patrie…". The shock of the sudden and brutal demise of this figurehead, chosen emissary of the King of Belgium, the nation's poet, was profound and the mourning heartfelt across Europe, including England. Verhaeren's body needed to be brought back to Flanders to his chosen resting place beside the Scheldt at Sint Amands, but in wartime such a journey was complicated and dangerous. Marthe and the painter Théo Van Rysselberghe, however, were determined to get Verhaeren home and so the extraordinary cortège with its attendant mourners commenced its journey across northern France, through hostile military terrain and across the border into Belgium.

In the rash of memorials in the wake of Verhaeren's death, one held at the Académie Française in Paris chose the great French poet Paul Valéry as its speaker. He said of his Belgian counterpart:

This is a great drama, gentlemen, we are living through, but this drama has found its poet. The competing themes of this life, between what has been and what might be, the disruption of nature and these deranged movements of men, found in Verhaeren their introduction, their master, their unique song. Through him our civilisation will have received the eminent dignity of lyrical expression.

II

From the very beginning until the last decade or so of his life, Verhaeren's poetry was in a state of evolution and flux. Unlike Rodenbach (whose poems are really one long meditation with Bruges and the dying canal towns of Flanders at their centre), or the Austrian poet Georg Trakl (1887-1914, whose subject range is narrow but of impressive visionary depth), Verhaeren's œuvre proceeds in a series of broad steps splashed with the gore of grief and the nectar of impetuous joy; existential challenges are forged from the paroxysm of crisis, cosmological ideals, a burgeoning socialism and the decisive upheavals in his personal life. Verhaeren remains robust and ritually enthusiastic, even in despair, and when in this state, he is able to record and comment on it from within its deepest recesses. The critic and poet Albert Mockel, who wrote an early biography of Verhaeren, believed that he possessed "a magic power to hypnotise himself". His vital  and expressively fluid poetry was later to act like cool oil on the overtaxed alexandrines of French poetry, and once he had turned his back on corrosive despair and suicidal impulses, his star was always directed towards life and its celebration without losing sight of its tragic propensity for pain and loss.

Verhaeren's first collection, *Les Flamandes* [The Flemish

Women, 1883], caused a minor scandal in staunchly Catholic Sint Amands. With its lusty Rubensesque content, it laid on a feast of earthy Flemish life or, as Zweig described it in his biography, "teeming with the exuberance of Rabelais". The poet's religiously pious family, appalled at the book's reception and fearing loss of face in the village, tried to prevent the printing of further copies but Verhaeren had already caused a stir; he had impressed the avant garde beyond the provinces, even though he was still something of an onlooker, an "energetic colourist" whose "wild stallions", as Zweig put it, were "still trotting along in the harness of the alexandrine."

The following collection was intriguing and perhaps unexpected. *Les Moines* [The Monks, 1886] was a step aside into a more rigid formal style and consisted of poems that Mockel described as "surrounded by a cold Parnassian light which turns them into an anonymous work, in spite of the poet's mark punched in many places over their surface." Childhood memories of the monastery at nearby Bornhem and the romantic mystery it evoked feed into an idealised view of monks, hair-shirted martyrs emerging from the ruins of history as symbols of a religious idealism. To get into character, Verhaeren even donned a monk's habit, wrote standing at a lectern and entered the monastery of Forges near Chimay for a few weeks to learn about the life there. Chilled by the austere conditions, however, he soon fled.

The following few years of Verhaeren's life, the late eighties, are marked by extreme mental torment and attendant ill-health, a favourable consequence of which was a major burst of poetic creativity. It was time for a rejection of the old order and a necessary tearing through into the modern, experimentation with free verse enabling his imaginative power to exploit his experience to the full – 'breakdown and breakthrough' one might term this period. During long periods of travel to Germany, Spain, Paris and London, Verhaeren allows himself to be overwhelmed by raw and exotic sensations, his morbid sensitivity further heightened by a strong infusion of Schopenhauer's philosophy. The death of his parents and estrangement from Catholicism leave his nerves raw. His mental state deteriorates as he endures self-imposed solitude in foreign places where, as a genuine *flâneur*, he welcomes the insatiable energy and anonymity of the crowd. He suffers digestive problems and, like Nietzsche, is sucked into a fetishist mania of physical self-regard caused by bad diet, alienation and nervous exhaustion. He travels again and again to London, lured by the febrile energy of the swollen metropolis and, on the very lip of the abyss, he manages to claw out three volumes of poetry. As Valéry put it: "Verhaeren returned from the hell of his heart and thought, bearer of the terrifying hides of the enemy that he had felled within himself." These volumes of bleak and often tortured poetry are generally cited by critics and readers today as amongst Verhaeren's strongest and most resilient work and stand alongside Maeterlinck's *Serres chaudes* [Hothouses, 1889] as the most important verses by Belgian hands to come out of that decade.

First came *Les Soirs* [The Evenings, 1887] followed by *Les Debacles* [The Debacles, 1888] and finally *Les Flambeaux noirs* [The Black Flames, 1891]; these three related collections became known later as *La Trilogie noire*, a label that has stuck. As Verhaeren later explained:

> They correspond to a state of physical sickness that I went through and where I worshipped pain for itself, in a kind of rage and savagery. *Les Soirs* sets the scene of a being who cries out, *Les Debacles* are the cry itself, *Les Flambeaux noirs* the reflection of the pain on general ideas which plague the afflicted one and which he deforms through his sickness and his abnormal personality.

He then admitted: "These three books have never been properly understood." What exactly he meant by this remains obscure, but what can be understood is that poems like 'Fatal Flower' and 'The Revolt' cradle an invocation to a poet's interior suffering worthy of Baudelaire. In 'Fatal Flower' for example, Verhaeren declares emphatically: "I want to stride towards madness and suns..." (p. 45) and in the last lines of 'The Revolt' the tension spills into a horrifying prospect which somehow recalls the acuminous anxiety of Poe or a frenzied scene from a Goya etching in the *Disasters of War* series:

The hour has come – yonder sounds the alarm;
against my door the rifle butts hammer
to kill, to be killed – what does it matter!
('The Revolt', p. 53)

One also sees the earliest examples of Verhaeren's delirious affirmations of the overpowering nature of life reaching through the gloom, as in the poem 'To Die':

> To die! Like overgrown flowers, to die!
> Too massive and too gigantic for life
>
> (p. 41)

while other poems, such as 'The Darkness', 'The Windmill' and 'The Frost' mirror, in monochrome, the poet's depressive affliction. Here, in 'The Frost', Verhaeren transmits the essence of a melancholy Flanders landscape held fast in the wires of an eternal winter:

> This evening, a vast open sky, abstract, supernatural,
> cold with stars, infinitely inaccessible…
>
> …and nothing to disturb the primal process,
> this reign of snow, bitter and corrosive.
>
> ('The Frost', p. 43)

Les Flambeaux noirs also contains the poem 'The Town', an extract of which is included in this volume, which looks ahead to a greater work to come – "The old dream is dead, the new is forged…" ('The Soul of the Town', p. 89).

After this time of crisis, Verhaeren entered a new phase in his personal life and his poetry. Following a prolonged courtship, he married Marthe Massin who was to dedicate her life to supporting him. Their love for each other lasted until Verhaeren's death in Rouen – and beyond, for Marthe never really recovered from her loss. Saved from mental collapse at the eleventh hour by Marthe, Verhaeren began to produce a series of works which moved away from the tormented and fiercely subjective, towards nature and the rapidly changing industrialized world at large. In *Les Campagnes hallucinées* [The Hallucinated Countryside, 1893] and the masterwork which followed in 1895, *Les Villes tentaculaires*, declamation rather than meditation germinates, the epic flexes its muscles and Hugolian words such as 'infinite', 'monstrous', 'gigantic' and 'eternal' appear with ever greater regularity, so much so that Aldous Huxley wryly observed that they "tend to mislay their power". Verhaeren's principal concerns, however, are the flood of people leaving the land for the cities, and the encroachment of these cities on the rural landscape he grew up in, a representation of which – in the rain, the snow, the wind and populated by rural labourers (including the ferryman, subject of one of Verhaeren's best-loved poems) – we are treated to in his next collection, *Les Villages illusoires* [The Illusory Villages, 1895]. *Les Campagnes hallucinées* presents a canvas of what the towns leave behind in the rural heartland – rats intent on devouring, wandering madmen and idiot stragglers weaving between the dykes and ponds of stagnant water, exemplified by the wonderfully observed poem 'The Beggars'. The poem 'The Town' (in which we see the town as vampirical devourer of the countryside) looks ahead to the ambitious and monumental *Les Villes tentaculaires* of 1895. Here Verhaeren's observations of industry and its unremitting, indifferent energy and toxic cacophony, of mercantilism and its accompanying vices, of the multitudinous population of the city, all consolidate in mighty poems which fall like Thor's hammer, such as 'The Soul of the Town' and 'The Plain'. While we have had glimpses of the sprawling gin-soaked London of carnality and scoured souls in earlier shorter poems such as 'London' from *Les Soirs*, and 'Shady Quarter' published posthumously, here the plaint is on a more grandiose scale, the cry more urgent, unflinching:

Unimaginable and criminal
the arms of hyperbolic machines
scything down the evangelic corn…

('The Plain', p. 85)

Verhaeren's new industrial cities were described by Valéry as "tentacled creatures whose body grows interminably, with unsettling activity, uncoordinated interior exchanges, incessant production of ideas, vices, luxury, political and artistic sensibilities that breed there, demanding a frenzied consuming of people, of living and thinking substance which they absorb and transform without rest." Surely there could hardly be a more accurate picture of the mega-urban metropolis of today. Although Verhaeren was aghast at the new industry's obliteration of the rural landscape, he nevertheless committed himself to a precarious optimism for the future, which largely explains his notable absence in the literary canon of post-war decades. Verhaeren determined to see in the infectious energies and rhythms of the new town a crucible for spiritual transformation or transcendence, a figurative communal energy channelled through heroic individual endeavour raising the consciousness of mankind.

In its visionary convulsion, *Les Villes tentaculaires* looks forward to the Expressionist poetry of the city, most notably by the Berlin poet Georg Heym, with his powerfully expressive poems such as 'Demons of the Cities' and 'God of the Town'. Elements of Verhaeren's vision are also expressed most forcibly by Heym's contemporary, the painter Ludwig Meidner in his 'Apocalyptic Landscape' series of 1912. Thanks to the efforts of Zweig and others, Heym would have read Verhaeren's works in translation in the first decade of the new century and have been influenced by his example. With imposing works like *Les Villes tentaculaires*, Verhaeren shows himself as a true pioneer of Modernism, as his form of life affirming, expressionistic poetry leads into the war-inspired apocalyptic incendiaries of Expressionism proper, and through to Eliot's *The Waste Land* a decade or so later. Verhaeren's yearning for humanity to somehow walk upright out of an industrial inferno that appeared to be consuming it, led almost inevitably towards socialism, which burgeoned as Zweig poetically put it "like a red blood drop upon his morbidly pallid poems". In the rapidly changing climate of the new century, Verhaeren's vision takes on the universality, the cosmic breathlessness for which he became known, giving rise to bold and dynamic poems that proclaim a transformation of values with varying degrees of success. His explicit fascination for humanity and its trajectory – what Robert Vivier called Verhaeren's optimistic *'mondialisme'* or world view, commences with *Les Visages de la vie* [The Faces of Life, 1899], and runs through the subsequent collections *Les Forces tumultueuses, La Multiple splendeur, Les Rythmes souverains* [The Sovereign Rhythms, 1910] and even into the posthumously published *Les Flammes hautes*. As Zweig explains in his biography, this final collection brings together a network of forces apparently separated from one another which are now revealed as having an ultimate cohesion: "In all manifestations of material life, he discovers the eternal forces: drunkenness, energy, triumph, joy, error, expectation, illusion. And these forces, or rather these forms of an essential force, animate all his poetry."

There is, however, an incongruity in Verhaeren's thought which both redeems him in an existential sense and also distorts the clarity of his vision. Verhaeren was acutely sensitive to mortality, but his yearning for human breakthrough rather than breakdown, and his will to transcend eternal human folly through creative energy, despite the poisoning effects, both spiritual and physical, of the onslaught of industrialism, prove fascinating, given the threshold to apocalyptic totalitarianism and holocaust he was unknowingly standing on. It is these unfortunate contradictions in his work that led to his poetry being neglected after the necessary radical recalibration of civilization following the First World War.

But looking back from a century later, it is hard not to admire Verhaeren's passion for life and protean dedication to all that grows and gains in strength. In his epic poem 'The Tree', for example, he undergoes a kind of inner transmogrification as his almost untenable enthusiasm and love for the tree fuse within him. As Zweig asserts, Verhaeren does not so much feel for his chosen subject in nature as actually becomes part of it; there is always an organic progression in his work, a slow and sure development which increases in strength as does a tree with each successive ring.

With the series *Toute la Flandre* [All Flanders] of 1908, we observe a more nostalgic, resigned and ageing Verhaeren irresistibly combing the natural world around him. Here are some of his most convincing non-epic works, intimate pieces replete with finely-observed detail and an impressionistic quality. Poems about life amongst the Flanders dunes, the sudden mood changes of the sea, the plight of the poor but proud fishermen are all particularly moving. They present a document of a rural coastal life lived in constant fear of loss at sea, a hard life lived close to nature, but an authentic one long since vanished under the monolithic concrete edifices of property developers:

> Yet nevertheless the tiny lights
> still keep watch from the cottages;
> scattered amongst the dark enclosures
> like crumbs of hope.
>
> ('The Danger', p. 119)

In the collection dedicated to Arthur Symons, *Les Villes à pignons* [The Gabled Towns, 1909] there are a number of dark-hued, haunting poems evoking the abandoned ports and the quays of the Flanders canal towns, the last saline breath of the dead cities of Bruges, Courtrai, Oudenarde, or even the some-what healthier lungs of Antwerp. Not surprisingly these poems seem to drift closer to the territory of Rodenbach, wounds of a once-animated place with their melancholy dressings. In the poem 'The Ship' from *Les Rhythmes souverains* [The Sovereign Rhythms], we find Verhaeren steady at the helm of his mature lyrical gift, producing a Conrad-like narrative to open the poem whose imagery seems effortlessly conjured from experience:

> We were advancing, calmly, beneath the stars;
> the oblique moon wandered around the bright craft,
> and the white terracing of spars and sails
> laid upon the ocean its giant shadow.
>
> The cold purity of blazing night
> glinted in space and quivered on the water;
> you could see the Great Bear and Perseus
> high above, as if in a dazzling shadow circus.
>
> ('The Ship', p. 127)

One of the biggest surprises in Verhaeren's work viewed as a whole is the trilogy of extraordinary poems he wrote to express his especially deep love for Marthe. These much-admired 'Hours' poems occur at intervals from 1896 to 1911 and have been placed chronologically in the text of this collection. Perhaps more than any of his other work, these intimate love poems for Marthe seem as fresh as when they were penned. One can almost smell the plants and soil after a rain shower, touch the trellises of fruit and feel the breeze across the plot at Caillou-qui-bique on reading them. Not only are they moving in their honest unembroidered state, stark and unencumbered by any portentousness or sentimentality, but they harbour a fusing of nature (in this case the isolated cottage garden at Caillou) and the human condition:

And that I feel, before the coffin lid is nailed down,
on the pure white bed our hands enjoin
and beside my brow upon the pale cushions,
for a supreme moment your cheek rest.
                    ('The Evening Hours, XXVI', p. 131)

A few other poems seem to signal fraternally to those in the 'Hours' series. 'The Storm' from *Les Blés mouvants* [The Moving Corn, 1912) recalls an incident in an orchard at the onset of a storm. This simple everyday moment becomes poetry in the hands of Verhaeren, the open-hearted onlooker who, in communion with the universal soul of things, endows orchard, fruit and grasses with a life within and yet beyond their own reality. Here, in a deceptively simple poem, one finds both the affirmation of physical elemental life and of 'elsewhere' in the image of the "laughing fruit" after the storm has passed, a symbol perhaps for Verhaeren's own existence.

A Note on the Texts

Verhaeren, for better or worse, was a compulsive meddler in his own poems, constantly amending them at each new edition. This makes both a translator's and an editor's job something of a headache, however interesting such changes may be to scholars. Critics and admirers in Verhaeren's day were often nonplussed at these constant changes and many had reservations; even the ever-faithful Zweig implied there was no need to 'interfere' with the originals. The English critic Edmund Gosse was of the opinion that what had been good enough for twenty years ago was surely good enough now. The problem was that not all the changes were for the better; they sometimes seemed needlessly to dilute the unconscious freshness of the original image. However, the Brussels publishing house Labor is, true to its name, currently producing, laboriously and heroically, a new edition of all his works in a definitive series which displays all the different versions. As a critical source this is of course invaluable, but it does not provide easy or accessible reading, as one is impeded continually by footnotes and columns of alternative versions; readers of Verhaeren in French must still make their choice from the versions available. Unsurprisingly, the older editions are more likely to be the original (or closer to the original) versions, whereas newer editions tend to be the last version Verhaeren left behind. For this collection I have used whichever versions seemed the stronger. For example I have used the originals of poems from *Les Villes tentaculaires* since later versions omit whole sections and in certain places tend to smooth out the imaginative creases that in the original lent a richer complexion. For instance, there is a section in the poem 'The Plain' where Verhaeren evokes brilliantly the body of a worker being absorbed into the machine:

> Their eyes, they are the eyes of the machine,
> their backs bend beneath it and their spines,
> their determined fingers, that complicate
> a thousand fingers precise and metallic...
>
> ('The Plain', p. 85)

which, in later versions, is watered down so that the whole frenzied image of fingers merging into the infinite cogs or bobbins is sadly lost. Having conferred with curators at the Verhaeren museum in Sint Amands as well as with one of the editors of

the Labor editions, Professor Michel Otten, about the different
versions I have taken the path indicated above, for better or
worse, at the same time feeling the need to inform readers that
alternatives exist should they wish to seek them out.

Will Stone

[1] Excerpt from the funeral address for Verhaeren by Francis Vielé-Griffin.
[2] From Marx, Jacques, *Verhaeren: biographie d'une œuvre* (Académie
Royale de langue et de littérature françaises, 1996).
[3] From Zweig, Stefan, *Errinerungen an Emile Verhaeren* (1917).
[4] Zweig, *op. cit.*

EMILE VERHAEREN
POEMS

'Place your strength in accord with those destinies
that the crowd, without knowing,
promulgates, in this night of illuminated anguish.'

EMILE VERHAEREN

CUISSON DU PAIN

Les servantes faisaient le pain pour les dimanches,
Avec le meilleur lait, avec le meilleur grain,
Le front courbé, le coude en pointe hors des manches,
La sueur les mouillant et coulant au pétrin.

Leurs mains, leurs doigts, leur corps entier fumait de hâte,
Leur gorge remuait dans les corsages pleins.
Leurs deux poings monstrueux pataugeaient dans la pâte
Et la moulaient en ronds comme la chair des seins.

Le bois brûlé se fendillait en braises rouges
Et deux par deux, du bout d'une planche, les gouges
Dans le ventre des fours engouffraient les pains mous.

Et les flammes, par les gueules s'ouvrant passage,
Comme une meute énorme et chaude de chiens roux,
Sautaient en rugissant leur mordre le visage.

EN HIVER

Le sol trempé se gerce aux froidures premières,
La neige blanche essaime au loin ses duvets blancs,
Et met, au bord des toits et des chaumes branlants,
Des coussinets de laine irisés de lumières.

Passent dans les champs nus les plaintes coutumières,
A travers le désert des silences dolents,
Où de grands corbeaux lourds abattent leurs vols lents
Et s'en viennent de faim rôder près des chaumières.

Mais depuis que le ciel de gris s'était couvert,
Dans la ferme riait une gaieté d'hiver,
On s'assemblait en rond autour du foyer rouge,

BAKING BREAD

The serving maids were making the Sunday bread,
with the best milk, the best grain,
brow bent, elbows bared from the sleeves to a point,
moistened by sweat running into the mixture.

Their hands, fingers, whole bodies smoking with haste,
their throats trembling in their full blouses.
Their two monstrous fists squelched in the dough
and moulded it into rounds like the flesh of breasts.

The burnt wood cracked to red embers
and two by two, on the end of a board, the gouges
shoved the soft bread into the oven's belly.

And the flames, forcing a passage through mouths
like a monstrous pack of blazing red dogs
leapt, roaring to bite at the bread's face.

IN WINTER

Sodden ground chapped by the first frosts,
white snow spreads its white quilt to the distance,
and lays, along roofs and ramshackle thatch,
a padding of wool, iridescent with light.

Over bare fields comes the habitual lament,
across the desert of mournful silences,
where giant crows beat their slow wings
and advance starving, to prowl around the cottages.

But since the sky was blanketed in grey,
in the farmstead chuckled winter's mirth,
for all were gathered there around the red hearth,

Et l'amour s'éveillait, le soir, de gars à gouge,
Au bouillonnement gras et siffleur, du brassin
Qui grouillait, comme un ventre, en son chaudron d'airain.

AUX MOINES

Moines venus vers nous des horizons gothiques,
Mais dont l'âme, mais dont l'esprit meurt de demain,
Qui reléguez l'amour dans vos jardins mystiques
Pour l'y purifier de tout orgueil humain,
Fermes, vous avancez par les routes des hommes,
Les yeux hallucinés par les feux de l'enfer,
Depuis les temps lointains jusqu'au jour où nous sommes,
Dans les âges d'argent et les siècles de fer,
Toujours du même pas sacerdotal et large.
Seuls vous survivez grands au monde chrétien mort,
Seuls sans ployer le dos vous en portez la charge
Comme un royal cadavre au fond d'un cercueil d'or.
Moines – oh! les chercheurs de chimères sublimes
Vos cris d'éternité traversent les tombeaux,
Votre esprit est hanté par la lueur des cimes,
Vous êtes les porteurs de croix et de flambeaux
Autour de l'idéal divin que l'on enterre.

Oh! les moines vaincus, altiers, silencieux,
Oh! les géants debout sur les bruits de la terre,
Qui n'écoutez que le seul bruit que font les cieux;
Moines grandis parmi l'exil et les défaites,
Moines chassés, mais dont les vêtements vermeils
Illuminent la nuit du monde, et dont les têtes
Passent dans la clarté des suprêmes soleils,
Nous vous magnifions, nous les poètes calmes.
Et puisque rien de fier n'est aujourd'hui vainqueur,
Puisqu'on a rabattu vers la fange les palmes,

36

and love awoke, at evening, between lad and lass
to the bubbling, whistling thickness of the brew
that seethed like a stomach in its bronze cooking pot.

TO THE MONKS

Monks approaching us from gothic horizons,
whose soul, whose spirit of tomorrow dies,
who confine love to your mystic gardens
to purify it of all human pride,
resolute, you advance down the roads of men,
eyes deluded by the fires of perdition
from distant times to our present day,
through ages of silver and centuries of iron,
and ever the same step pious and broad.
Alone, majestic, you survive a dead Christian world,
Alone with back unbowed you bear its load
like a royal corpse sunk in a coffin of gold.
Monks – seekers of sublime chimeras
your cries of eternity penetrate the necropolis,
your spirit is haunted by the glow of summits,
you are the bearers of cross and flame
around the divine ideal buried in the earth.

O monks, vanquished, unbowed, silenced,
O giants who tower above the din of the world,
who hear the only sound that heaven forged;
monks grown tall in exile and enslavement,
monks hunted down, but whose ruby garments
illumine the world's night, and whose heads
fade in the lucidity of supreme suns,
we, the peaceful poets, we magnify your forms.
And whilst no pride today is victor,
and palm leaves are trodden into the muck,

Moines, grands isolés de pensée et de cœur,
Avant que la dernière âme ne soit tuée,
Mes vers vous bâtiront de mystiques autels
Sous le vélum errant d'une chaste nuée,
Afin qu'un jour cette âme aux désirs éternels,
Pensive et seule et triste au fond de la nuit blême,
De votre gloire éteinte allume encor le feu,
Et songe à vous encor quand le dernier blasphème
Comme une épée immense aura transpercé Dieu!

LONDRES

Et ce Londres de fonte et de bronze, mon âme,
Où des plaques de fer claquent sous des hangars.
    Où des voiles s'en vont, sans Notre-Dame
Pour étoile, s'en vont, là-bas, vers les hasards.

Gares de suie et de fumée, où du gaz pleure
Ses spleens d'argent lointain vers des chemins d'éclair,
    Où des bêtes d'ennui bâillent à l'heure
Dolente immensément, qui tinte à Westminster.

Et ces quais infinis de lanternes fatales,
Parques dont les fuseaux plongent aux profondeurs,
    Et ces marins noyés, sous des pétales
De fleurs de boue où la flamme met des lueurs.

Et ces châles et ces gestes de femmes soûles,
Et ces alcools en lettres d'or jusques au toit.
    Et tout à coup la mort parmi ces foules,
O mon âme du soir, ce Londres noir qui traîne en toi!

monks, great solitaries of thought and heart
before the last soul becomes extinct,
my verses will build you mystic altars
beneath the wandering veil of a chaste cloud,
that one day this soul in eternal desire,
pensive, lonely, despairing, in the depths of pale night,
will rekindle the fire of your extinguished glory,
will dream of you still when the final blasphemy
like an immense sword skewers God.

LONDON

This London of cast-iron and bronze, my soul,
where under shed-roofs sheets of metal clang;
    where sailing ships disappear, without Notre Dame
for star, disappear, out there, towards fate.

Stations of soot and smoke, where the gas weeps
its spleens of distant silver towards paths of light
    where beasts of boredom yawn at the hour
that chimes, immensely mournful, from Westminster.

And this unending embankment of deadly lamps,
the fates whose spindles dive to the depths;
    and these drowned mariners, beneath petals
of mud flowers where the flame casts its glimmers.

And these gestures of drunken women and these shawls,
this liquor in golden letters high as roofs,
    and suddenly death amongst these multitudes,
O my evening soul, this dark London that drags in you.

LE MOULIN

Le moulin tourne au fond du soir, très lentement,
Sur un ciel de tristesse et de mélancolie,
Il tourne et tourne, et sa voile, couleur de lie,
Est triste et faible et lourde et lasse, infiniment.

Depuis l'aube, ses bras, comme des bras de plainte,
Se sont tendus et sont tombés; et les voici
Qui retombent encor, là-bas, dans l'air noirci
Et le silence entier de la nature éteinte.

Un jour souffrant d'hiver sur les hameaux s'endort,
Les nuages sont las de leurs voyages sombres,
El le long des taillis qui ramassent leurs ombres,
Les ornières s'en vont vers un horizon mort.

Sous un ourlet de sol, quelques huttes de hêtre
Très misérablement sont assises en rond:
Une lampe de cuivre est pendue au plafond
Et patine de feu le mur et la fenêtre.

Et dans la plaine immense et le vide dormeur
Elles fixent – les très souffreteuses bicoques! –
Avec les pauvres yeux de leurs carreaux en loques,
Le vieux moulin qui tourne et, las, qui tourne et meurt.

MOURIR

Un soir plein de pourpres et de fleuves vermeils
Pourrit, par au-delà des plaines diminuées.
Et fortement, avec les poings de ses nuées,
Sur l'horizon verdâtre, écrase des soleils.
Saison massive! Et comme octobre, avec paresse
Et nonchaloir, se gonfle et meurt dans ce décor
Pommes! caillots de feu; raisins! chapelets d'or,

THE WINDMILL

In the depth of evening the windmill turns, so slowly,
against a sky dejected and melancholy,
it turns and it turns and its sails are the colour of dregs
sad and weak, leaden and weary, endlessly.

Since dawn, its arms, like arms of lament,
have stretched and fallen; and here they are
fallen again, out there, in the darkened ether
and the absolute silence of lifeless nature.

Over the hamlets a suffering day of winter turns to slumber,
clouds are wearied from their sullen journeying,
and along the shrubbery where their shadows throng,
the ruts lead on towards a dead horizon.

Beneath the hem of the ground, a few beech huts
in a circle miserably squat;
from the ceiling hangs a lamp of copper
that lends the fire's sheen to window and plaster.

In the vast plain and slumbering emptiness
they stare out – the rickety hovels –
with the pauper eyes of their tattered tiles
at the old windmill that turns, weary, turns and dies.

TO DIE

An evening brimming with purples, rivers of crimson
putrefies above the enfeebled plains,
and powerfully, with the fists of its clouds
pulverises suns upon a green-tinged horizon.
Monumental season! Like October, with indolence
and unconcern, swells and expires in this scenery
apples! clots of fire; grapes! golden rosaries,

Que le doigté tremblant des lumières caresse,
Une dernière fois, avant l'hiver. Le vol
Des grands corbeaux? il vient. Mais aujourd'hui, c'est l'heure
Encor des feuillaisons de laque – et la meilleure.

Les pousses des fraisiers ensanglantent le sol.
Le bois tend vers le ciel ses mains de feuilles rousses
Et du bronze et du fer sonnent, là-bas, au loin.
Une odeur d'eau se mêle à des senteurs de coing
Et des parfums d'iris à des parfums de mousses.
Et l'étang plane et clair reflète énormément
Entre de fins bouleaux, dont le branchage bouge,
La lune, qui se lève épaisse, immense et rouge,
Et semble un beau fruit mûr, éclos placidement.

Mourir ainsi, mon corps, mourir, serait le rêve!
Sous un suprême afflux de couleurs et de chants,
Avec, dans les regards, des ors et des couchants,
Avec, dans le cerveau, des rivières de sève.
Mourir ! comme des fleurs trop énormes, mourir!
Trop massives et trop géantes pour la vie!
La grande mort serait superbement servie
Et notre immense orgueil n'aurait rien à souffrir!
Mourir, mon corps, ainsi que l'automne, mourir!

LE GEL

Ce soir, un grand ciel clair, surnaturel, abstrait,
Froid d'étoiles, infiniment inaccessible
A la prière humaine, un grand ciel clair paraît.
Il fige en son miroir l'éternité visible.

Le gel étreint cet infini d'argent et d'or,
Le gel étreint, les vents, la grève et le silence

which quivering fingers touch with light caresses
one last time, before winter. The flight
of the great crows? It's coming. But now is still the hour
of lacquered leafage – and it's the finest.

Sprouting of strawberries bloodies the ground,
the wood reaches her russet hands to the sky
as out there, in the distance, bronze and iron sound;
an aroma of water mingles with the scent of quince,
and the marrying perfumes of moss and iris.
The pond, flat, clear, reflects immensely,
between slender birches with stirring branches
the heavily-rising moon, huge and red,
that appears as a lovely ripened fruit, gently emerging.

To die like this, my body, to die, would be my dream.
Beneath a sovereign inrush of shades and songs
with, in glances, golds and sunsets
with, in the brain, rivers of sap.
To die! Like overgrown flowers, to die!
Too massive and too gigantic for life.
Mighty death would be amply furnished
and our great pride immune from anguish.
To die, my body. Like autumn, to die!

THE FROST

This evening, a vast open sky, abstract, supernatural,
cold with stars, infinitely inaccessible
to human prayer, a vast open sky emerges
to fix in its mirror visible eternity.

The frost grips this infinity of silver and gold
the frost grips, the winds, the silence and the shore,

43

Et les plaines et les plaines; le gel qui mord
Les lointains bleus, où les astres pointent leur lance.

Silencieux, les bois, la mer et ce grand ciel
Et sa lueur immobile et dardante!
Et rien qui remuera cet ordre essentiel
Et ce règne de neige acerbe et corrodante.

Immutabilité totale. On sent du fer
Et des étaux serrer son cœur morne et candide;
Et la crainte saisit d'un immortel hiver
Et d'un grand Dieu soudain, glacial et splendide.

FLEUR FATALE

L'absurdité grandit comme une fleur fatale
Dans le terreau des sens, des cœurs et des cerveaux.
Plus rien, ni des héros, ni des sauveurs nouveaux;
Et nous restons croupir dans la raison natale.

Je veux marcher vers la folie et les soleils,
Ses blancs soleils de lune au grand midi, bizarres,
Et ses lointains échos mordus de tintamarres
Et d'aboiements, là-bas, et pleins de chiens vermeils.

Lacs de rosés, ici, dans la neige, nuage
Où nichent des oiseaux dans des plumes de vent;
Grottes de soir, avec un crapaud d'or devant,
Et qui ne bouge et mange un coin de paysage.

Becs de hérons, énormément ouverts pour rien,
Mouche, dans un rayon, qui s'agite, immobile:
L'inconscience gaie et le tic-tac débile
De la tranquille mort des fous, je l'entends bien!

and the plains and the plains; the frost that bites
the blue distances, where the stars point their lances.

Silent, the woods, the sea and this sky so vast,
its motionless glimmer darting across,
and nothing to disturb the primal process,
this reign of snow, bitter and corrosive.

Immutability complete. You feel the iron tighten
and vices close on a heart mournful and open;
and you are seized by the fear of an immortal winter
and of a sudden mighty God, glacial and splendid.

FATAL FLOWER

Absurdity grows like a fatal flower
in the compost of senses, of brains and hearts.
Nothing more, no heroes, no fresh saviours;
and we remain rotting in native reason.

I want to stride towards madness and suns,
white suns of moon at the strike of noon, bizarre,
and distant echoes bitten by uproar
and baying, beyond, filled with ruby-red hounds.

Here, in the snow, lakes of rose, cloud
where birds nest in feathers of wind;
before caverns of evening, a golden toad
who never moves and gulps a patch of scenery.

Beaks of herons, opening wide for nothing,
in a beam, a fly now restless, now still:
joyful unconsciousness and the deranged ticking
of the madman's quiet death, I hear it well!

MES DOIGTS

Mes doigts, touchez mon front et cherchez, là,
Les vers qui rongeront, un jour, de leur morsure,
Mes chairs; touchez mon front, mes maigres doigts, voilà
Que mes veines déjà, comme une meurtrissure
Bleuâtre, étrangement, en font le tour, mes las
Et pauvres doigts – et que vos longs ongles malades
Battent, sinistrement, sur mes tempes, un glas,
Un pauvre glas, mes lents et mornes doigts!

Touchez, ce qui sera les vers, mes doigts d'opale,
Les vers, qui mangeront, pendant les vieux minuits
Du cimetière, avec lenteur, mon cerveau pâle,
Les vers, qui mangeront et mes dolents ennuis
Et mes rêves dolents et jusqu'à la pensée
Qui lentement incline, à cette heure, mon front,
Sur ce papier, dont la blancheur, d'encre blessée,
Se crispe aux traits de ma dure écriture.

Et vous aussi, mes doigts, vous deviendrez des vers,
Après les sacrements et les miséricordes,
Mes doigts, quand vous serez immobiles et verts,
Dans le linceul, sur mon torse, comme des cordes;
Mes doigts, qui m'écrivez, ce soir de rauque hiver,
Quand vous serez noués – les dix – sur ma carcasse
Et que s'écrasera sous un cercueil de fer,
Cette âpre carcasse, qui déjà casse.

LE GLAIVE

Quelqu'un m'avait prédit, qui tenait une épée
Et qui riait de mon orgueil stérilisé:
Tu seras nul, et pour ton âme inoccupée
L'avenir ne sera qu'un regret du passé.

MY FINGERS

My fingers stroke my brow and search there
for rhymes which, one day, with their bite, will eat into
my flesh; stroke my brow, skeletal fingers, there
already are my veins, like a bluish bruise,
they circle strangely, my poor weary fingers –
and how those long sickly nails beat
ominously against my temples, tolling,
tolling, my slow and mournful fingers!

You touch what will be verse, my opal fingers,
verse which will, at the graveyard's witching hour,
sluggishly devour my pale brain,
verse which will devour my dreary boredom
my dreary dreams right up to the thought
which at that hour slowly bends my brow
upon this paper, whose whiteness, wounded with ink,
tenses with the lines of my harsh writing.

And you too, my fingers, you'll be verse
after the sacraments and forgiveness,
my fingers, when you are stilled and turn green
under the shroud, laid upon my breast, like wires;
my fingers, writing to me this rough winter night,
when you're knotted – all ten – on my carcass
crushed there beneath a casket of iron,
this bitter carcass, already broken.

THE BLADE

Holding a sword and laughing
at my purified pride, someone predicted:
you'll be nothing, and for your vacant soul
the future holds only regret for the past.

Ton corps, où s'est aigri le sang de purs ancêtres,
Fragile et lourd, se cassera dans chaque effort:
Tu seras le fiévreux ployé, sur les fenêtres,
D'où l'on peut voir bondir la vie et ses chars d'or,

Tes nerfs t'enlaceront de leurs fibres sans sèves
Tes nerfs! – et tes ongles s'amolliront d'ennui,
Ton front, comme un tombeau dominera tes rêves,
Et sera ta frayeur, en des miroirs, la nuit.

Te fuir! – si tu pouvais! mais non, la lassitude
Des autres et de toi t'aura voûté le dos
Si bien, rivé les pieds si fort, que l'hébétude
Détrônera ta tête et plombera tes os.

Eclatants et claquants, les drapeaux vers les luttes.
Ta lèvre exsangue hélas! jamais ne les mordra:
Usé, ton cœur, ton morne cœur, dans les disputes
Des vieux textes, où l'on taille comme en un drap.

Tu t'en iras à part et seul – et les naguères
De jeunesse seront un inutile aimant
Pour tes grands yeux lointains – et les joyeux tonnerres
Chargeront loin de toi, victorieusement!

LA COURONNE

Et je voudrais aussi ma couronne d'épines
Et pour chaque pensée, une, rouge, à travers
Le front, jusqu'au cerveau, jusqu'aux frêles racines
Où se tordent les maux et les rêves forgés
En moi, par moi. Je la voudrais comme une rage,
Comme un buisson d'ébène en feu, comme des crins
D'éclairs et de flammes, peignés de vent sauvage;

Your body, where the blood of pure ancestors has soured,
frail and leaden, with each endeavour will be broken,
you'll be the restless stooping figure at the windows
from where you'll see life spring with its chariots of gold.

Your nerves will enlace you with sapless fibres,
your nerves! And your nails will soften with boredom,
your brow will rule your dreams like a tomb
and night in the mirrors, your nocturnal terror.

To escape yourself! – if you could! But no, your lassitude
and that of others will have bent your back
so surely, fastened your feet so firmly, that stupor
will dethrone your mind and seal your bones with lead.

Blazing and chattering, flags advance towards struggles,
alas, your bloodless mouth will never bite on them:
Threadbare, your heart, your sorrowful heart, in quarrels
with ancient texts, where one trims away as if at cloth.

You'll go on, isolated, alone – and the not so distant
time of youth will be a futile magnet
for your huge faraway eyes – and the joyful thunder
will charge on far from you, and conquer!

THE CROWN

Yes, I too would like my crown of thorns
and one for each thought, red hot, across
my brow, right into my brain, to the frail roots
where sins and forged dreams writhe
within me, through me. I crave it like a fury,
like an ebony bush in flame, like manes
of lightning and flames combed by a savage wind;

Et ce seraient mes vains et mystiques désirs,
Ma science d'ennui, mes tendresses battues
De flagellants remords, mes chatoyants vouloirs
De meurtre et de folie et mes haines têtues
Qu'avec ses dards et ses griffes, elle mordrait.
Et, plus intimement encor, mes anciens râles
Vers des ventres, mufles de lourdes toisons d'or,
Et mes vices de doigts et de lèvres claustrales
Et mes derniers tressauts de nerfs et de sanglots
Et, plus au fond, le rut même de ma torture,
Et tout enfin! O couronne de ma douleur
Et de ma joie, ô couronne de dictature
Debout sur mes deux yeux, ma bouche et mon cerveau,
O la couronne en rêve à mon front somnambule,
Hallucine-moi donc de ton absurdité;
Et sacre-moi ton roi souffrant et ridicule.

PIEUSEMENT

La nuit d'hiver élève au ciel son pur calice.

Et je lève mon cœur aussi, mon cœur nocturne,
Seigneur, mon cœur! vers ton pâle infini vide,
Et néanmoins je sais que tout est taciturne
Et qu'il n'existe rien dont ce cœur meurt, avide;
Et je te sais mensonge et mes lèvres te prient

Et mes genoux; je sais et tes grandes mains closes
Et tes grands yeux fermés aux désespoirs qui crient,
Et que c'est moi, qui seul, me rêve dans les choses
Sois de pitié. Seigneur, pour ma toute démence.
J'ai besoin de pleurer mon mal vers ton silence!…

La nuit d'hiver élève au ciel son pur calice!

and these would be my vain and mystic cravings,
my science of boredom, my beaten affections
of flagellant remorse, my shimmering desires
of murder and madness, my stubborn hates
that with sting and claw it would bite.
And more intimate still, my old death rattles
towards bellies, muffled in heavy fleeces of gold,
my flawed fingers and claustral lips,
my last jolting of nerves and sobs
and deeper, even the carnal rut of my torment,
until finally! crown of my agony
and of my joy, crown of tyranny
seated above my two eyes, my mouth and brain,
dream-crown on my sleepwalker's brow,
madly transfix me then with your absurdity;
and crown me your farcical long-suffering king.

PIOUSLY

Winter's night lifts to the sky its pure chalice.

And I lift my heart too, my nocturnal heart,
Lord, my heart! towards your pale empty infinite.
But still I know that everything is taciturn
and that nothing exists of which this heart dies, greedy;
and I know you lie and to you my lips pray

and my knees; I pray; I know your great clasped hands
and your great eyes closed to despairs that cry out,
and know that it's me who alone dreams myself in things:
have pity, Lord, for my consummate madness.
I need to weep my evil towards your silence…

Winter's night lifts to the sky its pure chalice.

51

LA REVOLTE

Vers une ville au loin d'émeute et de tocsin,
Où luit le couteau nu des guillotines,
En tout à coup de fou désir, s'en va mon cœur.

Les sourds tambours de tant de jours
De rage tue et de tempête,
Battent la charge dans les têtes.

Le cadran vieux d'un beffroi noir
Darde son disque au fond du soir,
Contre un ciel d'étoiles rouges.

Des glas de pas sont entendus
Et de grands feux de toits tordus
Echevèlent les capitales.

Ceux qui ne peuvent plus avoir
D'espoir que dans leur désespoir
Sont descendus de leur silence.

Dites, quoi donc s'entend venir
Sur les chemins de l'avenir,
De si tranquillement terrible?

La haine du monde est dans l'air
Et des poings pour saisir l'éclair
Sont tendus vers les nuées.

C'est l'heure où les hallucinés
Les gueux et les déracinés
Dressent leur orgueil dans la vie.

C'est l'heure – et c'est là-bas que sonne le tocsin;
Des crosses de fusils battent ma porte;
Tuer, être tué – qu'importe.

THE REVOLT

Towards a distant town of riot and alarm
where the naked blade of the guillotine shines,
with a sudden mad desire, my heart goes forth.

The dull drumbeats of so many days
of storm and silent rage,
sound the attack in every brain.

On the dark belfry the old clock face
beams its disc to evening's depths
against a firmament of crimson stars.

A death's knell of footsteps resounds
and the great light of distorted roofs
confuses the capitals.

They who could secure no further
hope than in their own despair
stepped down from their silence.

Tell me then, what do we hear coming
along the paths of the future
and all so casually terrible?

The world's hate in the ether
and fists to seize the lightning
stretched out towards the clouds.

The hour has come when the hallucinated,
the destitute and the uprooted
plant their pride upon existence.

The hour has come – yonder sounds the alarm;
against my door the rifle butts hammer
to kill, to be killed – what does it matter!

FINALE – LA MORTE

En sa robe, couleur de feu et de poison,
Le cadavre de ma raison
Traîne sur la Tamise.

Des ponts de bronze, où les wagons
Entrechoquent d'interminables bruits de gonds
Et des voiles de bateaux sombres
Laissent sur elle, choir leurs ombres.

Sans qu'une aiguille, à son cadran, ne bouge,
Un grand beffroi masqué de rouge,
La regarde, comme quelqu'un
Immensément de triste et de défunt.

Elle est morte de trop savoir,
De trop vouloir sculpter la cause,
Dans le socle de granit noir,
De chaque être et de chaque chose.
Elle est morte, atrocement,
D'un savant empoisonnement.
Elle est morte aussi d'un délire
Vers un absurde et rouge empire.

Ses nerfs ont éclaté.
Tel soir illuminé de fête,
Qu'elle sentait déjà le triomphe flotter
Comme des aigles, sur sa tête.
Elle est morte n'en pouvant plus,
L'ardeur et les vouloirs moulus,
Et c'est elle qui s'est tuée,
Infiniment exténuée.

Au long des funèbres murailles,
Au long des usines de fer
Dont les marteaux tannent l'éclair,
Elle se traîne aux funérailles.

FINALE – THE CORPSE

In her dress, colour of fire and poison
the corpse of my reason
drags down the Thames.

Bridges of bronze, where coaches clatter
with the ceaseless clanking of hinges
and the sails of sullen craft
over her let their shadows pass.

Without a moving hand on its dial
a great belfry, masked in crimson
regards her, like someone
immensely sunk in grief and loss.

She is dead for knowing too much,
from an excessive desire to sculpt the cause
in the pedestal of dark granite,
of every being and every object.
She is dead, horrifically,
of an ingenious poisoning.
Dead too from a journey of delirium
towards an absurd red kingdom.

Her nerves are shattered,
some evening lit by celebrations
when she already felt triumph glide
above her head like eagles.
She is dead of exhaustion,
her ardour and her will ground to dust
and it's she who killed herself,
endlessly worn out.

Along the gloomy walls,
along factories of iron
whose hammers tan the lightning flash
she drags herself to her funeral.

Ce sont des quais et des casernes,
Des quais toujours et leurs lanternes.
Immobiles et lentes filandières
Des ors obscurs de leurs lumières:
Ce sont des tristesses de pierres,
Maisons de briques, donjons en noir
Dont les vitres, mornes paupières,
S'ouvrent dans le brouillard du soir;
Ce sont de grands chantiers d'affolement,
Pleins de barques démantelées
Et de vergues écartelées
Sur un ciel de crucifiement.

En sa robe de joyaux morts, que solennise
L'heure de pourpre à l'horizon,
Le cadavre de ma raison
Traîne sur ta Tamise.

Elle s'en va vers les hasards
Au fond de l'ombre et des brouillards,
Au long bruit sourd des tocsins lourds,
Cassant leur aile, au coin des tours.
Derrière elle, laissant inassouvie
La ville immense de la vie;
Elle s'en va vers l'inconnu noir
Dormir en des tombeaux de soir,
Là-bas, où les vagues lentes et fortes,
Ouvrant leurs trous illimités,
Engloutissent à toute éternité :
Les mortes.

These are the quays and the barracks,
always the quays and their lanterns,
motionless, slow spinners
of the veiled gold of their lights;
these are the sorrows of stones,
houses of brick, keeps in darkness
whose windows, downcast eyelids,
are opened in evening's mists;
these are the great dockyards of panic,
crammed with dismantled ships
and dismembered yard-arms
against a sky of crucifixion.

In her dress of dead jewels, solemnized
by the purple hour on the horizon,
the corpse of my reason
drags down the Thames.

She sets out towards chances,
to the depths of shadows and fogs,
through the dull sound of the lowering bells,
breaking their wing on the corners of towers.
Behind her leaving unappeased
the sprawling town of life;
she sets out for the dark unknown,
to sleep in evening's tombs,
out there, where waves slow and strong
open their boundless chasms,
swallow for all eternity –
the dead.

LA VILLE (EXTRAIT)

La ville au loin s'étale et domine la plaine
Comme un nocturne et colossal espoir;
Elle surgit: désir, splendeur, hantise;
Sa clarté se projette en lueurs jusqu'aux cieux,
Son gaz myriadaire en buissons d'or s'attise,
Ses rails sont des chemins audacieux
Vers le bonheur fallacieux
Que la fortune et la force accompagnent;
Ses murs se dessinent pareils à une armée
Et ce qui vient d'elle encor de brume et de fumée
Arrive en appels clairs vers les campagnes.

C'est la ville tentaculaire,
La pieuvre ardente et l'ossuaire
Et la carcasse solennelle.

Et les chemins d'ici s'en vont à l'infini
Vers elle.

LES MENDIANTS

Les jours d'hiver quand le froid serre
Le bourg, le clos, le bois, la fange,
Poteaux de haine et de misère,
Par l'infini de la campagne,
Les mendiants ont l'air de fous.

Dans le matin, lourds de leur nuit,
Ils s'enfoncent au creux des routes,
Avec leur pain trempé de pluie
Et leur chapeau comme la suie
Et leurs grands dos comme des voûtes
Et leurs pas lents rythmant l'ennui;
Midi les arrête dans les fossés

THE TOWN (EXCERPT)

In the distance the town spreads and dominates the plain
like some colossal and nocturnal hope;
she rears up: desire, grandeur, dread;
her light casts beams to the heavens,
her myriad lamps flare up in bushes of gold,
her rails are audacious pathways
towards a deceptive bliss
attended by fortune and force;
her walls are lined up like an army
and that which issues from her still in fog and smoke
in clear appeals reaches the country.

This is the tentacled town,
the impassioned octopus, the ossuary
and carcass of solemnity.

And the ways from here go on to infinity –
towards her.

THE BEGGARS

Winter days when cold grips
the burgh, the fold, the wood, the mire,
stakes of misery and of hate,
in open country that never ends,
the beggars have the look of madmen.

In the morning, still heavy with night,
they sink in holes in the roads,
their bread sodden with rain
and their hats like soot
and their great backs like arches
and their slow step in rhythm with boredom;
in the ditches noon halts them

Pour leur repas ou leur sieste;
On les dirait immensément lassés
Et résignés aux mêmes gestes;
Pourtant, au seuil des fermes solitaires,
Ils surgissent, parfois, tels des filous,
Le soir, dans la brusque lumière
D'une porte ouverte tout à coup.

Les mendiants ont l'air de fous.
Ils s'avancent, par l'âpreté
Et la stérilité du paysage,
Qu'ils reflètent, au fond des yeux
Tristes de leur visage;
Avec leurs hardes et leurs loques
Et leur marche qui les disloque,
L'été, parmi les champs nouveaux,
Ils épouvantent les oiseaux;
Et maintenant que décembre sur les bruyères
S'acharne et mord
Et gèle, au fond des bières,
Les morts,
Un à un, ils s'immobilisent
Sur des chemins d'église,
Mornes, têtus et droits,
Les mendiants, comme des croix.

Avec leur dos comme un fardeau
Et leur chapeau comme la suie,
Ils habitent les carrefours
Du vent et de la pluie.

Ils sont le monotone pas
– Celui qui vient et qui s'en va
Toujours le même et jamais las –
De l'horizon vers l'horizon.
Ils sont l'angoisse et le mystère
Et leurs bâtons sont les battants
Des cloches de misère
Qui sonnent à mort sur la terre.

for their repast or their doze;
one would think them immensely weary
and resigned to the same gestures;
yet, on the thresholds of lonely farms,
they sometimes spring up, like rogues,
at evening, in the sudden light
of a door abruptly opened.

The beggars have the air of madmen.
They advance, through the harshness
and sterility of the landscape
which is reflected in the depths of
the sorrowful eyes of their faces;
with their old clothes and their rags
and their walk that breaks them,
in summer, amidst the fresh fields,
they scare away the birds;
and now that, on the moors, December
tears and bites
and freezes the dead
to the depths of caskets,
one by one, they come to a stop
on the roads to the church,
bleak, stubborn and upright,
the beggars, like crosses.

With their backs like a burden
and their hats like soot
they inhabit the crossroads
of wind and rain.

They are the monotonous tread
– that which comes and goes
ever the same and never weary –
from horizon to horizon.
They are agony and mystery
and their sticks are the hammers
of misery's bells
that toll for death on the earth.

Aussi, lorsqu'ils tombent enfin,
Sèches de soif, troués de faim,
Et se terrent comme des loups,
Au fond d'un trou,
Ceux qui s'en viennent,
Après les besognes quotidiennes,
Ensevelir à la hâte leur corps
Ont peur de regarder en face
L'éternelle menace
Qui luit sous leur paupière, encor.

CHANSON DE FOU

Les rats du cimetière proche,
Midi sonnant,
Bourdonnent dans la cloche.

Ils ont mordu le cœur des morts
Et s'engraissent de ses remords.

Ils dévorent le ver qui mange tout
Et leur faim dure jusqu'au bout.

Ce sont des rats
Mangeant le monde
De haut en bas.

L'église ? – elle était large et solennelle
Avec la foi des pauvres gens en elle,
Et la voici anéantie
Depuis qu'ils ont, les rats,
Mangé l'hostie.

So, when they finally drop
parched with thirst, pierced by hunger
and go to ground like wolves,
at the bottom of a hole,
those who come
after the day's labour,
to bury their bodies in haste
are scared to look full face
at the eternal threat
that still glitters, beneath the lid.

MADMAN'S SONG

The rats of the nearby cemetery,
as midday sounds
are buzzing in the bell.

They have bitten the heart of the dead
and grow fattened on their regrets.

They devour the worm that eats all
and their hunger lasts for evermore.

These are rats
eating the world
from top to bottom.

The Church? – it was solemn and broad
with the faith of the poor within,
and here it is laid waste
since the rats, they have
eaten the host.

Les blocs de granit se déchaussent
Les niches d'or comme des fosses
S'entrouvrent vides;
Toute la gloire évocatoire
Tombe des hauts piliers et des absides
Au son des glas.

Les rats,
Ils ont rongé les auréoles bénévoles,
Les jointes mains
De la croyance aux lendemains,
Les tendresses mystiques
Au fond des yeux des extatiques
Et les lèvres de la prière
Sur les bouches de la misère;
Les rats,
Ils ont rongé le bourg entier
De haut en bas,
Comme un grenier.

Aussi
Que maintenant s'en aillent
Les tocsins fous ou les sonnailles
Criant pitié, criant merci,
Hurlant, par au-delà des toits,
Jusqu'aux échos qui meuglent,
Nul plus n'entend et personne ne voit:
Puisqu'elle est l'âme des champs,
Pour bien longtemps,
Aveugle.

Et les seuls rats du cimetière proche,
A l'angélus hoquetant et tintant,
Causent avec la cloche.

Blocks of granite work loose,
the niches gold like graves
gape empty;
all the evocative glory
falls from high pillars and apses
at the sound of the death knell.

The rats
they have worn away the benevolent halos
the clasped hands
of belief in the future,
the mystical tenderness
deep in the eyes of the ecstatic
and the kisses of prayer
on the mouths of the destitute,
the rats
they have devoured the whole town
from top to bottom
like a granary.

So
just as they now die away
the mad alarms, the little bells
crying pity, crying mercy,
howling, over the roofs,
as far as the echoes sound,
no-one hearkens and no-one sees:
since it is the soul of the fields
for so long
blind.

And only the rats of the nearby cemetery
at the spluttering and tinkling of the angelus
converse with the bell.

LA NEIGE

La neige tombe, indiscontinûment,
Comme une lente et longue et pauvre laine,
Parmi la morne et longue et pauvre plaine,
Froide d'amour, chaude de haine.

La neige tombe, infiniment,
Comme un moment –
Monotone – dans un moment;
La neige choit, la neige tombe,
Monotone, sur les maisons
Et les granges et leurs cloisons;
La neige tombe et tombe
Myriadaire, au cimetière, au creux des tombes.

Le tablier des mauvaises saisons,
Violemment, là-haut, est dénoué;
Le tablier des maux est secoué
A coups de vent, sur les hameaux des horizons.

Le gel descend, au fond des os,
Et la misère, au fond des clos,
La neige et la misère, au fond des âmes;
La neige lourde et diaphane,
Au fond des âtres froids et des âmes sans flamme,
Qui se fanent, dans les cabanes.

Aux carrefours des chemins tors,
Les villages sont seuls, comme la mort;
Les grands arbres, cristallisés de gel,
Au long de leur cortège par la neige,
Entrecroisent leurs branchages de sel.
Les vieux moulins, où la mousse blanche s'agrège,
Apparaissent, comme des pièges.
Tout à coup droits, sur une butte:
En bas, les toits et les auvents
Dans la bourrasque, à contre vent,
Depuis novembre, luttent;
Tandis qu'infiniment la neige lourde et pleine
Choit, par la morne et longue et pauvre plaine.

THE SNOW

Unceasingly, the snow falls,
an endless, plodding, wretched skein,
onto the mournful, endless wretched plain,
frozen with love, burning with hatred.

Endlessly, the snow falls,
like a moment –
monotonous – in a moment;
the snow falls, the snow drops,
monotonous, on the houses,
on the barns and their walls;
the snow falls and falls
smothering the cemetery, the hollows of tombs.

Apron of ill-starred seasons,
on high, violently loosened;
apron of evils shaken
by gusts over hamlets on horizons.

Frost descends, deep in the bone,
and wretchedness to the depths of the fold,
snow and wretchedness deep in the soul;
snow, weighted and diaphanous,
deep in cold hearths and unlit souls,
that wither away in the hovels.

At the crossroads of twisting tracks,
villages in solitude, like death;
great trees, spangled with frost,
along their cortege through the snow,
interweave their salty boughs.
Old windmills, where white moss collects,
appear like traps,
suddenly erect, on a mound;
below, the canopies and roofs
in the squall, against the wind
since November, struggle on;
while endlessly the snow, full and weighted
drops to the endless plain drear and wretched.

Ainsi s'en va la neige au loin,
En chaque sente, en chaque coin.
Toujours la neige et son suaire,
La neige pâle et inféconde,
En folles loques vagabondes,
Par à travers l'hiver illimité du monde.

LA PLUIE

Longue comme des fils sans fin, la longue pluie
Interminablement, à travers le jour gris,
Ligne les carreaux verts avec ses longs fils gris,
Infiniment, la pluie,
La longue pluie,
La pluie.

Elle s'effile ainsi, depuis hier soir,
Des haillons mous qui pendent,
Au ciel maussade et noir.
Elle s'élire, patiente et lente,
Sur les chemins, depuis hier soir,
Sur les chemins et les venelles,
Continuelle.

Au long des lieues,
Qui vont des champs vers les banlieues.
Par les routes interminablement courbées,
Passent, peinant, suant, fumant,
En un profil d'enterrement,
Les attelages, bâches bombées;
Dans les ornières régulières
Parallèles si longuement
Qu'elles semblent, la nuit, se joindre au firmament,
L'eau dégoutte, pendant des heures:

Thus the snow departs into the distance,
in every corner, on every path,
always the snow and its shroud,
the snow, barren and pale,
in roaming rags of madness
across the boundless winter of the world.

THE RAIN

Long as interminable threads, the long rain
endlessly through the grey day,
lines the green pane with her long threads of grey,
infinitely, the rain,
the long rain,
the rain.

Since last evening she's frayed,
hanging with rags all sodden,
in a sky sombre and sullen.
Since last evening, she's become unravelled,
patient and slow, down the lanes,
down the lanes and the alleyways,
endlessly.

For many a league,
from fields to suburbs,
along roads relentlessly bending,
grieving, sweating, smoking, they go by,
an outline of burial against the sky,
teams yoked, tarpaulins bulging;
down uniform ruts
parallel for such a length
they seem at night to reach the firmament,
water drips, down the long hours;

Et les arbres pleurent et les demeures,
Mouillés qu'ils sont de longue pluie,
Tenacement, indéfinie.

Les rivières, à travers leurs digues pourries,
Se dégonflent sur les prairies,
Où flotte au loin du foin noyé;
Le vent gifle aulnes et noyers;
Sinistrement, dans l'eau jusqu'à mi-corps,
De grands bœufs noirs beuglent vers les cieux tors;

Le soir approche, avec ses ombres,
Dont les plaines et les taillis s'encombrent,
Et c'est toujours la pluie
La longue pluie
Fine et dense, comme la suie.

La longue pluie,
La pluie – et ses fils identiques
Et ses ongles systématiques
Tissent le vêtement,
Maille à maille, de dénûment,
Pour les maisons et les enclos
Des villages gris et vieillots:
Linges et chapelets de loques
Qui s'effiloquent,
Au long de bâtons droits;
Bleus colombiers collés au toit;
Carreaux, avec, sur leur vitre sinistre.
Un emplâtre de papier bistre;
Logis dont les gouttières régulières
Forment des croix sur des pignons de pierre;
Moulins plantés uniformes et mornes,
Sur leur butte, comme des cornes:

Clochers et chapelles voisines,
La pluie,
La longue pluie.
Pendant l'hiver, les assassine.

the trees weep and the homesteads,
dampened as they are by the long rain,
tenacious, undefined.

Rivers, through their rotten dykes
across the meadows seep away
where far off drifts the drowned hay;
the wind slaps walnut and alder;
sinister, waist-high in water,
huge black oxen bellow at a contorted sky.

Evening draws on, with her shadows,
burdening the copses and plains,
and forever the rain,
the long rain,
fine yet dense like soot.

The long rain,
the rain – its identical threads
and methodical fingernails
weave the garment,
stitch by stitch, of deprivation,
for the houses and the folds
villages grey and old:
linen and rosaries of rags
that fray
along the upright posts;
blue dovecots fixed to roofs;
windows on whose sinister panes,
layers of paper blackish brown;
dwellings whose gutters quite uniform
make crosses on gables of stone;
windmills set, identical and dreary,
atop their mounds like horns;

Steeples and side chapels,
the rain,
the long rain,
all winter long murders them.

La pluie,
La longue pluie, avec ses longs fils gris.
Avec ses cheveux d'eau, avec ses rides,
La longue pluie
Des vieux pays,
Eternelle et torpide!

LE VENT

Sur la bruyère longue infiniment,
Voici le vent cornant novembre,
Sur la bruyère, infiniment.
Voici le vent
Qui se déchire et se démembre,
En souffles lourds, battant les bourgs,
Voici le vent,
Le vent sauvage de novembre.

Aux puits des fermes.
Les seaux de fer et les poulies
Grincent;
Aux citernes des fermes.
Les seaux et les poulies
Grincent et crient
Toute la mort, dans leurs mélancolies.

Le vent rafle, le long de l'eau,
Les feuilles mortes des bouleaux,
Le vent sauvage de novembre
Le vent mord, dans les branches,
Des nids d'oiseaux;
Le vent râpe du fer
Et peigne, au loin, les avalanches,
Rageusement, du vieil hiver,

The rain,
the long rain, with its long grey threads,
its watery locks and wrinkled skin.
The long rain
of the old country,
languorous, everlasting!

THE WIND

Over the boundless moor,
here is the wind announcing November,
over the moor, endlessly,
here is the wind
that tears itself from limb to limb
in heavy breaths, battering the burghs,
here is the wind
the wild wind of November.

In the wells of farms
the pails of iron and pulleys
are creaking;
to the tanks of farmsteads.
The pails and pulleys
creak and cry
of death, in their melancholy.

Along the water, the wind makes off with
the dead leaves of birches,
the wild wind of November;
the wind bites, in the branches,
the nests of birds;
the wind, a rasp of iron
furiously combs the distant avalanches,
of old winter,

Rageusement, le vent,
Le vent sauvage de novembre.

Dans les étables lamentables.
Les lucarnes rapiécées
Ballottent leurs loques falotes
De vitres et de papier.
– Le vent sauvage de novembre! –
Sur sa butte de gazon bistre,
De bas en haut, à travers airs,
De haut en bas, à coups d'éclairs,
Le moulin noir fauche, sinistre,
Le moulin noir fauche le vent.
Le vent,
Le vent sauvage de novembre.

Les vieux chaumes, à cropetons,
Autour de leurs clochers d'église,
Sont ébranlés sur leurs bâtons;
Les vieux chaumes et leurs auvents
Claquent au vent.
Au vent sauvage de novembre.
Les croix du cimetière étroit,
Les bras des morts que sont ces croix.
Tombent, comme un grand vol,
Rabattu noir, contre le sol.

LE SILENCE

Depuis l'été que se brisa sur elle
Le dernier coup d'éclair et de tonnerre,
Le silence n'est point sorti
De la bruyère.

furiously, the wind,
the wild wind of November.

In the pitiful cowsheds
the patched-up skylights
toss their puny rags
of pane and paper.
– The wild wind of November! –
On its mound of yellowing brown grass,
from low to high, through flows of air,
from high to low, with lightning bolts,
the black windmill darkly scythes,
the black windmill scythes the wind,
the wind,
the wild wind of November.

The old thatched roofs, crouched
all around the church bells,
are shaken on their poles;
the old thatched roofs and their canopies
chatter to the wind,
to the wild wind of November.
The crosses of the cramped cemetery,
the arms of the dead are these crosses
falling like a great spread of wings,
darkly folded, against the earth.

THE SILENCE

Since summer broke over it
the last lightning bolt, thunderclap,
the silence has never left
the moor.

Autour de lui, là-bas, les clochers droits
Secouent leur cloche, entre leurs doigts,
Autour de lui, rôdent les attelages,
Avec leur charge à triple étage,
Autour de lui, aux lisières des sapinières,
Grince la roue en son ornière,
Mais aucun bruit n'est assez fort
Pour déchirer l'espace intense et mort.

Depuis l'été de tonnerres chargé.
Le silence n'a pas bougé,
Et la bruyère, où les soirs plongent
Par au delà des montagnes de sable
Et des taillis infinissables,
Au fond lointain des loins, l'allonge.

Les vents mêmes ne remuent point les branches
Des vieux mélèzes, qui se penchent
Là-bas, où se mirent, en des marais.
Obstinément, ses yeux abstraits;
Seule le frôle, en leurs voyages,
L'ombre muette des nuages
Ou quelquefois celle, là-haut,
D'un vol planant de grands oiseaux.

Depuis le dernier coup d'éclair rayant la terre,
Rien n'a mordu, sur le silence autoritaire.
Ceux qui traversèrent sa vastitude.
Qu'il fasse aurore ou crépuscule,
Ont subi tous l'inquiétude
De l'inconnu qu'il inocule.
Comme une force ample et suprême.
Il reste, indiscontinûment, le même:
Des murs obscurs de sapins noirs
Barrent la vue au loin vers des sentiers d'espoir;
De grands genévriers songeurs
Effraient les pas des voyageurs;
Des sentes complexes comme des signes

All around it, out there, the upright towers,
shake their bells between their fingers,
around it, harnesses rasp,
with their three-tier high-stacked load,
around it at the edge of the firs,
the wheel creaks in its rut,
but no noise has the strength
to pierce a space so powerful and dead.

Since the summer of heavy thunder,
the silence has not stirred
and the moor, where evenings plunge
over mountains of sand
and boundless brush
stretches to the furthest distance.

Even the winds fail to stir the branches
of old larches, that incline
yonder, mirrored in the marshes,
defiant and abstract their eyes;
alone in their journeys,
the silent shadows of clouds,
graze it, or sometimes, high above
a gliding flight of great birds.

Since the last lightning fork rent the earth,
nothing has bitten on the authoritarian silence.
Those who traversed its vastness,
whether at dawn or close of day,
all have suffered the dread disquiet
of the unknown that it inoculates.
Like a prodigal and sovereign force
it prevails, unceasingly, unchanged;
the sombre walls of black firs
deny a view to the distance, towards paths of hope;
as giant dreaming junipers
frighten the footfalls of travellers;
and intricate paths like signs

S'entremêlent, en courbes et lignes malignes,
Et le soleil déplace, à tout moment,
Les mirages, vers où s'en va l'égarement.

Depuis l'éclair par l'orage forgé,
L'âpre silence, aux quatre coins de la bruyère,
N'a point changé.

Les vieux bergers que leurs cent ans disloquent
Et leurs vieux chiens, usés et comme en loques,
Le regardent, parfois, dans les plaines sans bruit,
Sur les dunes en or que les ombres chamarrent.
S'asseoir, immensément, du côté de la nuit.
Alors les eaux ont peur, au pli des mares,
La bruyère se voile et blêmit toute,
Chaque feuillée, à chaque arbuste, écoute
Et le couchant incendiaire
Tait, devant lui, les cris brandis de sa lumière.

Et les hameaux qui l'avoisinent,
Sous les chaumes de leurs cassines,
Ont la terreur de le sentir, là-bas,
Dominateur, quoique ne bougeant pas;
Mornes d'ennui et d'impuissance,
Ils se tiennent, sous sa présence,
Comme aux aguets – et redoutent de voir,
A travers les brumes qui se desserrent,
Soudainement, s'ouvrir, dans la lune, le soir,
Les yeux d'argent de ses mystères.

interweave in curves and crafty lines,
and constantly the sun displaces mirages
towards which distractedly she moves.

Since the lightning forged by the storm,
the bitter silence in all four corners of the moor
has not changed at all.

The old shepherds, broken by their hundred years
and their old dogs, worn out like rags,
gaze on it sometimes, over soundless plains
on dunes of gold bedecked with shadow.
It sits, in vastness, at the edge of night.
In the creases of ponds, waters have taken fright,
the moor is veiled, and all grows pale,
each leaf to each shrub hearkens
and before it the flaming sunset
stifles the brandished cries of its light.

And the villages close by,
beneath the thatch of their roofs
are in dread of sensing it, out there,
the all-powerful, that which does not move;
doleful with boredom and impotence,
they are rooted there, held by its presence,
as if keeping watch, in dread of seeing,
suddenly, through loosening mists,
in the moon, at evening,
the silver eyes of its mysteries.

Le passeur d'eau, les mains aux rames,
A contre flot, depuis longtemps,
Luttait, un roseau vert entre les dents.

Mais celle hélas! qui le hélait
Au delà des vagues, là-bas,
Toujours plus loin, par au delà des vagues,
Parmi les brumes reculait.

Les fenêtres, avec leurs yeux,
Et le cadran des tours, sur le rivage.
Le regardaient peiner et s'acharner.
En un ploiement de torse en deux
Et de muscles sauvages.

Une rame soudain cassa
Que le courant chassa,
A vagues lourdes, vers la mer.

Celle là-bas qui le hélait.
Dans les brumes et dans le vent, semblait
Tordre plus follement les bras.
Vers celui qui n'approchait pas.

Le passeur d'eau, avec la rame survivante,
Se prit à travailler si fort
Que tout son corps craqua d'efforts
Et que son cœur trembla de fièvre et d'épouvanté.

D'un coup brusque, le gouvernail cassa
Et le courant chassa
Ce haillon morne, vers la mer.

Les fenêtres, sur le rivage,
Comme des yeux grands et fiévreux
Et les cadrans des tours, ces veuves
Droites, de mille en mille, au bord des fleuves,

THE FERRYMAN

The ferryman, hands to oars,
so long against the waves,
struggled on, a green reed between his teeth.

But she, alas, who hailed him
beyond the waves, yonder,
ever further, there beyond the waves
receded into the mists.

The windows, with their eyes,
the towers' dials on the bank,
watched him toil and strain so hard,
his whole body bent in half,
his wild muscles.

Suddenly an oar broke
which the current drove,
on rapid waves, towards the sea.

And out there, she who hailed him
in the winds and in the mists, seemed
to twist more madly her arms,
towards him who could not advance.

The ferryman, with surviving oar,
began to labour so hard
that his whole body cracked with effort
and his heart quivered with fever and terror.

With a sudden blow, the rudder broke
and the current drove
this mournful rag on towards the sea.

On the bank, windows
like immense febrile eyes
and the towers' dials, those widows
so upright, along the banks of the rivers,

81

Fixaient, obstinément,
Cet homme fou, en son entêtement
A prolonger son fol voyage.

Celle là-bas qui le hélait,
Dans les brumes, hurlait, hurlait,
La tête effrayamment tendue
Vers l'inconnu de l'étendue.

Le passeur d'eau, comme quelqu'un d'airain,
Planté, dans la tempête blême,
Avec l'unique rame, entre ses mains,
Battait les flots, mordait les flots quand même.
Ses vieux regards hallucinés
Voyaient les loins illuminés
D'où lui venait toujours la voix
Lamentable, sous les cieux froids.

La rame dernière cassa
Que le courant chassa
Comme une paille, vers la mer.

Le passeur d'eau, les bras tombants,
S'affaissa morne, sur son banc,
Les reins rompus de vains efforts,
Un choc heurta sa barque, à la dérive,
Il regarda, derrière lui, la rive:
Il n'avait pas quitté le bord.

Les fenêtres et les cadrans,
Avec des yeux béats et grands
Constatèrent sa ruine d'ardeur,
Mais le tenace et vieux passeur
Garda tout de même, pour Dieu sait quand,
Le roseau vert, entre ses dents.

were stubbornly fixed on
this crazed man, in his doggedness
to prolong his insane voyage.

She yonder who hailed him,
in the mists, was yelling, yelling,
her head terrifyingly stretched
towards the unknown vastness.

The ferryman, like a man of iron,
planted in the pale storm
a solitary oar between his hands,
battled, bit at the waves anyway.
The visionary with his timeworn gaze
searched the hallucinated space
from where the voice always came to him
forlorn, beneath cold skies.

The surviving oar broke
and the current drove it
like a straw, on towards the sea.

The ferryman, arms dropping,
slumped gloomily on his seat,
loins exhausted with futile strain,
all adrift, a shock hit the boat,
he glanced behind him at the bank:
he had never even left the edge.

The windows and the dials
with their huge wide-open eyes
noted his ruined ardour;
but the stalwart old ferryman
retained all the same, for only God knows when,
the green reed between his teeth.

LA PLAINE

La plaine est morne et ses chaumes et granges
Et ses fermes dont les pignons sont vermoulus,
La plaine est morne et lasse et ne se défend plus,
La plaine est morne et morte – et la ville la mange.

Formidables et criminels,
Les bras des machines hyperboliques,
Fauchant les blés évangéliques,
Ont effrayé le vieux semeur mélancolique
Dont le geste semblait d'accord avec le ciel.

L'orde fumée et ses haillons de suie
Ont traversé le vent et l'ont sali:
Un soleil pauvre et avili
S'est comme usé en de la pluie.

Et maintenant, où s'étageaient les maisons claires
Et les vergers et les arbres allumés d'or,
On aperçoit, à l'infini, du sud au nord,
La noire immensité des usines rectangulaires.

Telle une bête énorme et taciturne
Qui bourdonne derrière un mur,
Le ronflement s'entend, rythmique et dur,
Des chaudières et des meules nocturnes;
Le sol vibre, comme s'il fermentait
Le travail bout comme un forfait,
L'égout charrie une fange velue
Vers la rivière qu'il pollue;
Un supplice d'arbres écorchés vifs
Se tord, bras convulsifs,
En façade, sur le bois proche;
L'ortie épuise aux cœurs sablons et oche
Et les fumiers, toujours plus hauts, de résidus:
Ciments huileux, plâtras pourris, moellons fendus,
Au long de vieux fossés et de berges obscures
Lèvent, le soir, leurs monuments de pourritures.

THE PLAIN

The plain is dreary and its stubble-fields and barns
and with their worm-holed gables, the farms,
the plain is doleful, weary, can defend itself no longer,
the plain is doleful, dead and the town devours it.

Unimaginable and criminal
the arms of hyperbolic machines
scything down the evangelic corn,
have scared away the melancholy old sower
whose movement seemed in harmony with the heavens.

Smoky filth and its rags of soot
have crossed the wind and left their stain:
a sun impoverished and degraded
is worn down by the rain.

And now, where bright houses rose in terraces,
the orchards and trees lit with gold,
one sees, from south to north, into infinity,
the black immensity of rectangular factories.

Such a colossal and taciturn beast
bellowing on behind a wall,
the snoring is heard, rhythmic and harsh,
of boilers and nocturnal grind-stones;
the earth quivers as if fermenting,
and labour seethes like infamy,
a hairy mire that travels the sewer
is carried down to foul the river;
a torture of trees flayed alive,
convulsively twist their arms
in the lee of the wood close by;
nettles fade at the heart of ochre sands
and dung heaps, ever higher with swill:
rotting plaster, cracked rubble, greasy cement,
along old ditches and dismal embankments
raise, each evening, their monuments of filth.

Sous des hangars tonnants et lourds,
Les nuits, les jours,
Sans air et sans sommeil,
Des gens peinent loin du soleil:
Morceaux de vie en l'énorme engrenage,
Morceaux de chair fixée, ingénieusement,
Pièce par pièce, étage par étage,
De l'un à l'autre bout du vaste tournoiement.
Leurs yeux, ils sont les yeux de la machine,
Leurs dos se ploient sous elle et leurs échines,
Leurs doigts volontaires, qui se compliquent
De mille doigts précis et métalliques,
S'usent si fort en leur effort,
Sur la matière carnassière,
Qu'ils y laissent, à tout moment,
Des empreintes de rage et des gouttes de sang.

Dites! l'ancien labeur pacifique, dans l'août
Des seigles mûrs et des avoines rousses,
Avec les bras au clair, le front debout
Dans l'or des blés qui se retrousse
Vers l'horison torride où le silence bout.

Dites! le repos tiède et les midis élus,
Tressant de l'ombre pour les siestes.
Sous les branches, dont les vents prestes
Rythment, avec lenteur, les grands gestes feuillus,
Dites, la plaine entière ainsi qu'un jardin gras,
Toute folle d'oiseaux éparpillés dans la lumière,
Qui la chantent, avec leurs voix plénières,
Si près du ciel qu'on ne les entend pas.

Mais aujourd'hui, la plaine, elle est finie;
La plaine est morne et ne se défend plus:
Le flux des ruines et leurs reflux
L'ont submergée, avec monotonie.

Beneath oppressive and thunderous sheds,
day and night,
without air and without sleep,
people labour on far from the light:
scraps of life the enormous gearing,
scraps of flesh attached, ingeniously
room by room, floor by floor,
from one end to the other of the vast whirling.
Their eyes, they are the eyes of the machine,
their backs bend beneath it and their spines,
their determined fingers, that complicate
a thousand fingers precise and metallic
are worn down so hard in their toil
over flesh-eating matter,
that they'll leave there, at any time
beads of blood and imprints of fury.

Speak then of ancient peaceful labour, in the August
of ripened rye and auburn oats,
arms raised to the light and brow upheld
in the gold of the corn that rolls on
towards a torrid horizon where silence boils.

Speak then of blessed noons, mellow repose,
woven in shadows for siestas.
Beneath branches whose nimble breezes
lend slow rhythm to the great leaf motion,
speak then of the whole plain as a fecund garden,
in whose light is scattered a bedlam of birds,
who sing with voices in chorus
so close to the heavens they cannot be heard.

But today for the plain it's all over;
the plain is doleful and can defend itself no longer:
the flow of ruins and their backward surge
have submerged it in bleak monotony.

On ne rencontré, au loin, qu'enclos rapiécés
Et chemins noirs de houille et de scories
Et squelettes de métairies
Et trains coupant soudain des villages en deux.

Les Madones ont tu leurs voix d'oracle
Au coin du bois, parmi les arbres;
Et les vieux saints et leur socle de marbre
Ont chu dans les fontaines à miracles.

Et tout est là, comme des cercueils vides
Et détraqués et dispersés par l'étendue,
Et tout se plaint, ainsi que les défunts perdus
Qui sanglotent le soir dans la bruyère humide.

Hélas! la plaine, hélas! elle est finie!
Et ses clochers sont morts et ses moulins perclus.
La plaine, hélas! elle a toussé son agonie
Dans les derniers hoquets d'un angelus.

L'ÂME DE LA VILLE

Les toits semblent perdus
Et les clochers et les pignons fondus,
Dans ces matins fuligineux et rouges,
Où, feux à feux, des signaux bougent.

Une courbe de viaduc énorme
Longe les quais mornes et uniformes;
Un train s'ébranle immense et las.

Au loin, derrière un mur, là-bas,
Un steamer rauque avec un bruit de corne.

In the distance one sees only patched-up folds,
the blackened tracks of slag and coal,
skeletons of small holdings
and trains that abruptly cleave villages in two.

The Madonnas have silenced their oracle voice
at the wood's corner, amongst the trees;
and the old saints and their plinths of marble
have fallen into the fountain of miracles.

And all are there, like empty coffins,
ruined and scattered over far expanses
and all lament like the lost departed
who weep at evening in the damp heather.

Alas, the plain, alas! It's all over.
And its bells are lifeless and windmills lame.
The plain, alas! It has coughed its death throes
in the last gasp of the angelus.

THE SOUL OF THE TOWN

The roofs seem lost
and the bells and gables vague,
in these red and fuliginous dawns,
where, light by light, the signals change.

An immense viaduct's curve
borders quays dreary and uniform;
a train moves off vast and forlorn.

Out there, in the distance, behind a wall
a steamer hoarsely sounds its horn.

Et par les quais uniformes et mornes,
Et par les ponts et par les rues,
Se bousculent, en leurs cohues,
Sur des écrans de brumes crues,
Des ombres et des ombres.

Un air de soufre et de naphte s'exhale;
Un soleil trouble et monstrueux s'étale;
L'esprit soudainement s'effare
Vers l'impossible et le bizarre;
Vivants ou morts, voit-il encor
Ce qui se meut en ces décors,
Où, devant lui, sur les places, s'élève
Le dressement tout en brouillards
D'un tombeau d'or ou d'un palais blafard
Pour il ne sait quel géant rêve?

Ô les siècles et les siècles sur cette ville,
Grande de son passé
Sans cesse ardent – et traversé,
Comme à cette heure, de fantômes!
Ô les siècles et les siècles sur elle,
Avec leur vie infatigable et criminelle
Battant, depuis quels temps?
Chaque demeure et chaque pierre
De désirs fous et de colères carnassières!

Quelques huttes d'abord et quelques prêtres:
L'asile à tous, l'église et ses fenêtres
Laissant filtrer la lumière du dogme sûr
Et sa naïveté vers les cerveaux obscurs.
Donjons dentés, palais massifs, cloîtres barbares;
Croix des papes dont le monde s'empare;
Moines, abbés, barons, serfs et vilains;
Mitres d'orfroi, casques d'argent, vestes de lin;
Luttes d'instincts, loin des luttes de l'âme,
Entre voisins, pour l'orgueil vain d'une oriflamme;
Haines de sceptre à sceptre et monarques faillis

And along the quays dreary and uniform,
along the bridges and along the streets,
jostling each other in their throngs,
upon screens of raw mists
shadows and more shadows.

An air of sulphur and naphtha is exhaled,
a monstrous and murky sun unfurled;
of a sudden the spirit is alerted
to the impossible and the fantastic;
living or dead, it still watches
what moves in these scenes,
where, on the squares before it, rises
the upright presence clothed in mists
of a pale pediment or a golden pillar
for who knows what giant chimera?

The centuries and centuries upon this town,
prodigious with her past
unceasingly fevered – and transversed,
now as in that time, by spectres!
The centuries and centuries upon it,
with their lives so criminal and tireless
beating still – but from what epoch? –
in every dwelling and every stone
crazed desires! carnivorous wrath!

At first some priests, a scattering of huts:
asylum for all, the church and all its glass
where the light of sure dogma and its lack of guile
filters through to unlit minds.
Vast palaces, barbaric cloisters, crenellated keeps;
papal crosses which the earth seizes;
abbots, barons, serfs, monks and miscreants;
gilded mitres, silver helmets, linen raiments;
struggles of instinct, far from spiritual struggles
between neighbours, for the vain pride of a banner;
hatred of sceptre to sceptre and failed rulers

Sur leur fausse monnaie ouvrant leurs fleurs de lys,
Taillant le bloc de leur justice à coups de glaive
Et la dressant et l'imposant: grossière et brève.

Puis, l'ébauche, lente à naître, de la cité:
Forces qu'on veut dans le droit seul planter;
Ongles du peuple et mâchoires de rois;
Mufles crispés dans l'ombre et souterrains abois
Vers on ne sait quel idéal au fond des nues;
Tocsins brassant, le soir, des rages inconnues;
Textes de délivrance et de salut, debout
Dans l'atmosphère énorme où la révolte bout;
Livres dont les pages, soudain intelligibles,
Brûlent de vérité, comme jadis les Bibles;
Hommes divins et clairs, tels des monuments d'or
D'où les événements sortent armés et forts;
Vouloirs nets et nouveaux, consciences nouvelles
Et l'espoir fou, dans toutes les cervelles,
Malgré les échafauds, malgré les incendies
Et les têtes en sang au bout des poings brandies.

Elle a mille ans la ville,
La ville âpre et profonde;
Et sans cesse, malgré l'assaut des jours,
Et les peuples minant son orgueil lourd,
Elle résiste à l'usure du monde.
Quel océan, ses cœurs! Quel orage, ses nerfs!
Quels nœuds de volontés serrés en son mystère!
Victorieuse, elle absorbe la terre,
Vaincue, elle est l'affre de l'univers;
Toujours, en son triomphe ou ses défaites,
Elle apparaît géante, et son cri sonne et son nom luit,
Et la clarté que fait sa face dans la nuit
Rayonne au loin, jusqu'aux planètes!

Ô les siècles et les siècles sur elle!

on fake coins flaunting their *fleurs de lys*,
cleaving their full justice with sweep of sword
erecting and imposing it, brief and crude.

Then, slow to emerge, the vague form of the town:
forces they want to fix only in law;
nails of the people and kings' jaws;
muzzles tensed in shadow, a subterranean howl
to who knows what ideal beyond the clouds;
at evening, alarms snaking, unknown ragings;
texts of deliverance and salvation planted
in the sprawling atmosphere where revolt boils;
books whose pages, of a sudden intelligible,
burn with truth, as in the of bibles of old;
men, brilliant and divine like monuments of gold
from whom spring actions armed and powerful;
clear and fresh cravings, a new consciousness
and crazed hope, in all those brains,
despite the scaffolds, despite the flames
and at the end of brandished fists the bloodied heads.

The town has known a thousand years,
grim is the town and deep;
and unceasingly, despite the assault of days,
and the people wearing down her weighty pride,
she resists the usury of the world.
What an ocean her hearts! What a storm her nerves!
What a snarl of will sealed in her mystery!
Victorious, she absorbs the earth;
vanquished, she is the scourge of the universe;
forever, in her triumphs and her defeats,
she appears a giant, her name, her cry rings out,
and the light that makes the gold of her lamps
beam into the distance, as far as the planets!

The centuries and centuries upon this town.

Son âme, en ces matins hagards,
Circule en chaque atome
De vapeur lourde et de voiles épars;
Son âme énorme et vague, ainsi que de grands dômes
Qui s'estompent dans le brouillard;
Son âme, errante, en chacune des ombres
Qui traversent ses quartiers sombres,
Avec une ardeur neuve au bout de leur pensée,
Son âme formidable et convulsée,
Son âme, où le passé ébauche
Avec le présent net l'avenir encor gauche.

Ô ce monde de fièvre et d'inlassable essor
Rué, à poumons lourds et haletants,
Vers on ne sait quels buts inquiétants?
Monde soumis pourtant à des lois d'or,
À des lois douces, qu'il ignore encore
Mais qu'il faut, un jour, qu'on exhume,
Une à une, du fond des brumes.
Monde aujourd'hui têtu, tragique et blême
Qui met sa vie et son âme dans l'effort même
Qu'il projette, le jour, la nuit,
À chaque heure, vers l'infini.

Ô les siècles et les siècles sur cette ville!

Le rêve ancien est mort et le nouveau se forge.
Il est fumant dans la pensée et la sueur
Des bras, fiers de travail, des fronts, fiers de lueurs,
Et la ville l'entend monter du fond des gorges
De ceux qui le portent en eux
Et le veulent crier et sangloter aux cieux.

Et de partout on vient vers elle,
Les uns des bourgs et les autres des champs,
Depuis toujours, du fond des loins;
Et les routes éternelles sont les témoins
De ces marches, à travers temps,

On these fretful mornings, her soul
roams in every atom
of dense haze and scattered veils;
her soul, amorphous and immense, like mighty domes
that soften in the mist.
Her soul is straying through every shadow
that crosses the gloomier quarters
to the limits of thought with renewed ardour,
her soul tremendous and contorted,
her soul, where the past shapes
the clear present with the ungainly future.

O, this world of fever and unflagging growth
rushed on with heavy gasping lungs
to who knows what disturbing conclusion?
The promised world still has its laws of gold,
gentle laws that it may yet ignore
but which must, one day, be exhumed
from the misty depths, one by one.
The world today is headstrong, tragic, pale
shackling life and soul to equal toil
that it projects, by day, by night,
at all hours, towards the eternal.

The centuries and centuries upon her!

The old dream is dead, the new is forged.
It smokes in thought and in the sweat
of arms proud of their work, of proudly glowing brows,
and the town hears it rise from the throats
of those who carry it deep within them
and yearn to cry out and lament to the heavens.

And from everywhere they move toward her,
some from the small towns, some from the fields,
since time immemorial, from the far distance
and the eternal roads are the witness
across time, of these processions,

95

Qui se rythment comme le sang
Et s'avivent, continuelles.

Le rêve! Il est plus haut que les fumées
Qu'elle renvoie envenimées
Autour d'elle, vers l' horizon;
Même dans la peur ou dans l'ennui,
Il est là-bas, qui domine, les nuits,
Pareil à ces buissons
D'étoiles d'or et des couronnes noires,
Qui s'allument, le soir, évocatoires.

Et qu'importent les maux et les heures démentes,
Et les cuves de vice où la cité fermente,
Si quelque jour, du fond des brouillards et des voiles,
Surgit un nouveau Christ, en lumière sculpté,
Qui soulève vers lui l'humanité
Et la baptise au feu de nouvelles étoiles.

LES HEURES CLAIRES

I

O notre joie
Qui s'illumine et flotte au vent dans l'air de soie!

Voici la maison douce et son pignon léger,
Et le jardin et le verger.

Voici le banc, sous les pommiers
D'où s'effeuille le printemps blanc
A pétales frôlants et lents.

which like blood, beat a rhythm,
continually reviving them.

The dream! it rises higher than the smoke
that she sends back poisoned
around her and towards the horizon;
even in fear, even in boredom
she is there, holding sway, night after night,
like those clusters
of golden stars and blackened crowns,
which flood the evening with redolent light.

And what matter the evil, the insane hours,
and vats of vice in which the town boils,
if some day from the depths of mist and veils,
a new Christ looms, in sculpted light,
who lifts humanity towards him
and in fresh star fire performs the baptism.

THE CLEAR HOURS

I

O our joy
which is illumined and floats on the wind in silken air.

Here is the gentle house and its light gable,
   the garden and the orchard.

   Here is the bench, beneath the apple trees
   where white springtime is shed
   with slow caressing petals.

Voici des vols de lumineux ramiers
    Planant, ainsi que des présages,
    Dans le ciel clair du paysage.

Voici, pareils à des baisers tombés sur terre
    De la bouche du frêle azur,
    Deux bleus étangs simples et purs,
Bordés naïvement de fleurs involontaires.

O la splendeur de notre joie et de nous-mêmes,
En ce jardin où nous vivons de nos emblèmes.

    III

Ce chapiteau barbare où des monstres se tordent,
Soudés entre eux à coups de griffes et de dents,
En un tumulte fou de sang, de cris ardents,
De blessures et de gueules qui s'entre-mordent,
C'était moi-même, avant que tu fusses la mienne
    O toi la neuve, ô toi l'ancienne!
Qui vins à moi, du fond de ton éternité
Avec, entre les mains, l'ardeur et la bonté.

Je sens en toi les mêmes choses très profondes
    Qu'en moi-même dormir,
    Et notre soif de souvenir
Boire l'écho, où nos passés se correspondent.

    Nos yeux ont dû pleurer aux mêmes heures
      Sans le savoir, pendant l'enfance;
    Avoir mêmes effrois, mêmes bonheurs,
      Mêmes éclairs de confiance;
    Car je te suis lié par l'inconnu
Qui me fixait, jadis, au fond des avenues
    Par où passait ma vie aventurière;
    Et, certes, si j'avais regardé mieux,
      J'aurais pu voir s'ouvrir tes yeux
      Depuis longtemps, en ses paupières.

Here are flights of luminous woodpigeons
      hovering, like omens,
      in the clear sky of the country.

Here, like kisses fallen on earth
      from the mouth of the fragile azure,
      two blue lakes simple and pure,
artlessly bordered by innocent flowers.

O the splendour of our joy and of ourselves,
in this garden where we live on with our insignia.

     III

This barbarous head where monsters writhe,
bound together by tooth and claw,
in a mad tumult of blood, of ardent cries,
of wounds and mouths that tear each other,
that was me, before you were mine,
      O, you the new, you the ancient one!
You, who came to me, from the depths of your eternity
bearing in your hands passion and goodness.

I feel in you the self-same depths
      that in my own self slumber,
      and in our thirst to remember
drink the echo, where our pasts come together.

    Our eyes must have wept at the same hour
      without our knowing, during childhood;
    with the same fears, same joys,
      same sparks of confidence;
    for I am linked to you by the unknown
that fixed me, once, from the depths of avenues
    where my adventurer's life was spent;
    and, of course, had I looked closer,
      I would have been able to see your eyes open
      long ago, beneath their lids.

XVIII

Au clos de notre amour, l'été se continue:
    Un paon d'or suit l'avenue
    Et traverse le gazon vert;
  Nos étangs bleus luisent, couverts
  Du baiser blanc des nénuphars de neige;
Aux quinconces nos groseilliers font des cortèges;
Un insecte de prisme irrite un cœur de fleur;
De merveilleux sous-bois se jaspent de lueurs;
Et, comme des bulles légères, mille abeilles,
Sur des grappes d'argent, vibrent au long des treilles.

    L'air est si beau qu'il paraît chatoyant;
    Sous les midis profonds et radiants,
On dirait qu'il remue en rosés de lumière;
    Tandis qu'au loin, les routes coutumières
Telles de lents gestes qui s'allongent vermeils,
A l'horizon nacré, montent vers le soleil.

Certes, la robe en diamants du bel été
Ne vêt aucun jardin d'aussi pure clarté,
Et c'est la joie unique éclose en nos deux âmes,
Qui reconnaît sa vie en ces bouquets de flammes.

UNE HEURE DU SOIR

Mon cœur? – Il est tombé dans le puits de la mort.
Et moi du bord de la margelle,
Du bord de la vie et de la margelle,
J'entends mon cœur lutter, dans le puits de la mort.

– Le silence est effrayant –

XVIII

In the garden of our love, summer moves on:
    a peacock of gold follows the avenue
    and traverses the green lawn;
they gleam, our blue ponds, covered
with the white kiss of snowy water lilies;
along staggered rows our redcurrants form processions;
an insect prism inflames a flower's heart;
wondrous undergrowth is marbled with gleams;
and, like airy bubbles, a thousand bees,
on clusters of silver, quiver along the vines.

    The air is so beautiful it seems to shimmer;
    beneath deep and radiant noontimes,
one would say it stirs into roses of light;
    whilst, in the distance, the familiar roads
that stretch out like slow gestures, ruby red
to pearl the horizon, climbing towards the sun.

Surely, lovely summer's diamond gown
can clothe no other garden with such brightness,
and this unique joy that blooms in our two souls,
in these bouquets of flame its own life recalls.

AN EVENING HOUR

My heart? It fell into the well of death.
and me on the very lip of the edge,
on the lip of life and the very edge,
I hear my heart struggle, in the well of death.

– The silence is terrifying –

101

Comme un morceau de gel
La lune aussi, au fond du puits
Laisse tomber sa pâleur éternelle.

Mon cœur est un quartier de chair,
Un bloc de viande saignante,
Mon cœur bat, seul, au fond du puits,
Contre un morceau de lune ardente.

– Le silence et le grand froid;
Et, par la nuit, le vague effroi
D'un ciel plein d'astres en voyage –

Au fond des citernes de mort,
Mon cœur s'acharne et bat encor
A coups de fièvre, sur la lune.
La lune, à lui, parmi les eaux s'allie;
La lune est un visage étincelant;
La lune est un visage aux regards blancs;
La lune est un bloc de folie;
La lune est une bouche de gel
Qui mord mon cœur essentiel.

Les tenailles des minuits clairs
Serrent ce cœur entre leurs fers;
La patience des aiguilles du givre
Criblent ce cœur ardent de vivre;
Déjà les eaux, couleur de son cadavre,
Roulent ce cœur, avec de lents remous
Et des hoquets, vers de grands trous.
Et certes, un soir, la lune enfermera
Ce cœur, malgré ses battements de haine,
Comme une pierre en une gaine.

Like a sliver of frost
the moon too, at the bottom of the well
lets fall her eternal pallor.

My heart is a cut of flesh,
a block of bloody meat,
alone, in the well's depths, my heart beats
against a sliver of ardent moon.

– Silence and the great chill;
and, through the night, the obscure dread
of a sky filled with journeying stars –

At the bottom of the tanks of death,
my heart battles on and still beats
with feverish blows, upon the moon.
Allied to it, amid the waters, is the moon;
the moon is a gleaming face;
the moon is a face of white glances;
the moon is a block of madness;
the moon is a mouth of ice
that bites my essential heart.

The pincers of clear midnights
seize this heart in their iron grip;
the patience-needles of frost
pierce this heart inflamed with life;
already the waters, the colour of its corpse,
roll this heart, with slothful eddies
and hiccoughs, towards great ditches.
But surely, one evening, the moon will immure
this heart, despite its thumpings of hate,
like a stone in a sheath.

UN MATIN

C'était, dans la campagne émerveillée, un coin
Où la prairie en fleur brillait comme un visage,
Où deux grands étangs bleus s'arrondissaient au loin
Comme un double baiser du ciel au paysage.

Sur les mousses de vair et les pierrailles d'or,
Les eaux, telles des pleurs d'aube s'égouttaient blanches;
L'éclair d'un vol d'oiseau frôlait le sol, l'essor
Rythmé, suivant le va-et-vient, au vent, des branches.

Des mélèzes frangés tendaient leurs bras ouverts
Comme des pèlerins tournés vers la lumière.
L'ombre dormait sous eux, au long des gazons verts,
Et s'étendait jusqu'aux miroirs de la rivière.

Les cristaux du matin étincelaient dans l'air;
Toute la vie ornait le silence des choses;
Toutes les feuilles brillaient de mouvement clair
Et le Verbe tremblait sur leurs lèvres décloses.

SUR LES GRÈVES

Sur ces plages de sel amer
Et d'âpre immensité marine,
Je déguste, par les narines,
L'odeur d'iode de la mer.

Quels échanges de forces nues
S'entre-croisent et s'insinuent,
Avec des heurts, avec des bonds,
A cette heure de vie énorme,
Où tout s'étreint et se transforme,
Les vents, les cieux, les flots, les monts!

ONE MORNING

It was in the wonder-filled countryside, a patch
where the flowering meadow shone like a face,
where two huge blue lakes widened to the distance
like a double kiss from sky to landscape.

Over mosses of vair and loose stones of gold,
the waters dripped white like tears of dawn;
the flash of a bird's wing caressed the ground, the flight
rhythmic, following the to and fro of branches on the wind.

The fringed larches extended their open arms
like pilgrims turning towards the light.
Beneath them, along green lawns, shadow slumbered
and spread as far as the river's mirrors.

The crystals of morning glinted in the air;
all life adorned the silence of things;
all leaves shone with a movement so clear
and on their parted lips quivered the Word.

ON THE SHORE

On the beaches of bitter salt
in the harsh vastness of the shore,
I savour, through my nostrils
the odour of iodine from the sea.

What exchanges of naked forces
intersect and insinuate themselves
with collisions, with leaps,
at that hour of monumental life
where all embraces and is transformed:
winds, mountains, waves, skies!

Et c'est fête dans tout mon être;
L'ardeur de l'univers
Me rajeunit et me pénètre.
Que m'importe d'avoir souffert,
D'avoir raclé mon cœur avec la chaîne
– Qui vient et va – de la douleur humaine,
Que m'importe! – je sens
Mon corps renouvelé vibrer de joie entière
Et se tremper vivant et saint
Dans ce brassin
De formidable et sauvage matière.

Le roc casse le flot, le flot ronge le roc.
Un silence se fait: le choc
Des gros tonnerres d'eau ébranlent les falaises;
Une île au loin se nourrit de la mer
Et monte d'autant plus que les grèves s'affaissent.
Le sable boit le soleil clair
– Oh revenir aux aurores du monde! –
Tout se confond, tout se détruit, tout se féconde.
On vit un siècle en un instant.

Et qu'importe ce deuil du temps:
La mort!
Sans elle
Jamais l'éternité n'apparaîtrait nouvelle;
Homme qui tue et qui engendre,
Il faut apprendre
A jouir de la mort.

La mort, la vie – et leur ivresse!
Oh toutes les vagues de la mer!
Cercueils fermés, berceaux ouverts,
Gestes d'espoir ou de détresse,
Les membres nus, le torse au clair,
Je m'enfonce soudain, sous vos caresses rudes,
Avec le désir fou
De m'en aller, un jour, jusqu'au bout,
Là-bas, me fondre en votre multitude!

Celebration floods my entire being:
the ardour of the universe
re-animates and penetrates me.
What matter to have suffered,
to have had my heart chafed with the chain
– now here, now gone – of human pain,
what matter! – I feel
my renewed body quiver replete with joy
to be dipped alive and holy
in this vat
of terrific and savage substance.

The rock breaks the wave, the wave wears the rock.
A silence is born: the blows
of mighty thunderclaps shake the cliffs;
a distant island is nourished by the sea
and rises ever more so as the shore sinks.
Bright sun the sand drinks…
– O to return to the dawns of the world –
all is confused, all destroys itself, all is enriched.
In a single second one lives a hundred years.

And what matters this mourning of time:
Death!
Without it
never would eternity appear so fresh;
man who kills and who gives life,
you must learn
to rejoice in death.

Death, life – and their intoxication!
O, all the waves of the ocean…
Sealed coffins, open cradles,
gestures of hope or distress,
limbs naked and bared chests,
I am suddenly, in your rough caress,
possessed with the insane desire
to set off one day, to the very end,
and out there lose myself in your multitude.

X

Toute croyance habite au fond de notre amour.
On lie une pensée ardente aux moindres choses:
A l'éveil d'un bourgeon, au déclin d'une rose,
Au vol d'un frêle et bel oiseau qui, tour à tour,
Arrive ou disparaît, dans l'ombre ou la lumière.
Un nid, qui se disjoint au bord moussu d'un toit
Et que le vent saccage, emplit l'esprit d'effroi.
Un insecte qui mord le cœur des fleurs trémières
Épouvante: tout est crainte, tout est espoir.
Que la raison, avec sa neige âpre et calmante,
Refroidisse soudain ces angoisses charmantes,
Qu'importe, acceptons-les sans trop savoir
Le faux, le vrai, le mal, le bien qu'elles présagent;
Soyons heureux de nous sentir enfants,
Pour croire à leur pouvoir fatal ou triomphant;
Et gardons-nous, volets fermés, des gens trop sages.

XXIX

Vous m'avez dit, tel soir, des paroles si belles
Que sans doute les fleurs qui se penchaient vers nous
Soudain nous ont aimés et que l'une d'entre elles,
Pour nous toucher tous deux, tomba sur nos genoux.

Vous me parliez des temps prochains où nos années,
Comme des fruits trop mûrs, se laisseraient cueillir;
Comment éclaterait le glas des destinées,
Et comme on s'aimerait, en se sentant vieillir.

Votre voix m'enlaçait comme une chère étreinte,
Et votre cœur brûlait si tranquillement beau
Qu'en ce moment j'aurais pu voir s'ouvrir sans crainte
Les tortueux chemins qui vont vers le tombeau.

THE AFTERNOON HOURS

X

All belief dwells in the heart of our love.
To the least thing we bind an ardent thought:
to the awakening of a bud, the decline of a rose,
to the flight of a frail and beautiful bird which, by turns
arrives or vanishes, in light or shadow.
A nest that comes apart at the roof's mossy edge
and that the wind wrecks, fills the spirit with dread.
An insect that bites at the hearts of hollyhocks
strikes fear: all is anguish, all is hope.
Let reason, with her bitter and soothing snow,
suddenly chill these charming torments,
what matter, let us accept them without knowing all
the false, the true, the evil, the good they portend;
let us be content to feel as children,
to believe in their power, fatal or triumphant;
and let us guard ourselves, shutters closed,
from those who think they know all.

XXIX

You said to me, one evening, words so lovely
that doubtless the flowers inclining towards us
suddenly loved us and one of their number,
to touch us both, dropped upon our knees.

You spoke to me of times to come when our years,
like over-ripe fruits, would let themselves be gathered in,
of how the knell of destinies would clearly ring,
how we would love each other, as we felt ourselves age.

Your voice enclosed me like a cherished embrace,
and your heart burned, so calmly beautiful
that in this moment, fearless, I might have seen loom
those tortuous roads that lead towards the tomb.

L'ARBRE

Tout seul,
Que le berce l'été, que l'agite l'hiver,
Que son tronc soit givré ou son branchage vert,
Toujours, au long des jours de tendresse ou de haine,
Il impose sa vie énorme et souveraine
Aux plaines.

Il voit les mêmes champs depuis cent et cent ans
Et les mêmes labours et les mêmes semailles;
Les yeux aujourd'hui morts, les yeux
Des aïeules et des aïeux
Ont regardé, maille après maille,
Se nouer son écorce et ses rudes rameaux.
Il présidait tranquille et fort à leurs travaux;
Son pied velu leur ménageait un lit de mousse;
Il abritait leur sieste à l'heure de midi
Et son ombre fut douce
A ceux de leurs enfants qui s'aimèrent jadis.

Dès le matin, dans les villages,
D'après qu'il chante ou pleure, on augure du temps;
Il est dans le secret des violents nuages
Et du soleil qui boude aux horizons latents;
Il est tout le passé debout sur les champs tristes,
Mais quels que soient les souvenirs
Qui, dans son bois, persistent,
Dès que janvier vient de finir
Et que la sève, en son vieux tronc, s'épanche,
Avec tous ses bourgeons, avec toutes ses branches,
– Lèvres folles et bras tordus –
Il jette un cri immensément tendu
Vers l'avenir.

Alors, avec des rais de pluie et de lumière,
Il frôle les bourgeons de ses feuilles premières,
Il contracte ses nœuds, il lisse ses rameaux;
Il assaille le ciel, d'un front toujours plus haut;
Il projette si loin ses poreuses racines

THE TREE

All alone,
whether cradled by summer, or tormented by winter,
whether its trunk be frosted or branches green,
through days of tenderness and of loathing
it forever imposes its vast and sovereign life
upon the plains.

For century on century it has seen the same pastures,
the same tilled fields, the same sowing times;
the eyes of those now dead, eyes
of grandparents and forebears
have watched, stitch by stitch
its bark and rugged branches form.
Over their work it presided, strong and calm;
its hairy bole furnished them a bed of moss;
it gave shelter for their noontime nap
and its shade was tender
to those of their children who once loved.

At daybreak, in the villages
after its sobbing or songs, the weather is foretold;
it's there in the secret of savage clouds
and the sun that sulks on hidden horizons;
it's the whole past standing on sorrowing fields,
but whatever the memories
enduring in its wood,
as soon as January draws to a close
and the sap, in its old trunk, rises,
with all its buds, with all its branches
– with wild lips and arms contorted –
it unleashes a cry, massive and far reaching
towards the future.

Then, with stokes of rain and light
the buds of its new leaves it lightly brushes,
it acquires its knurls, smooths its foliage;
it assails the sky with the loftiest of brows;
it projects its porous roots so far

Qu'il épuise la mare et les terres voisines
Et que parfois il s'arrête, comme étonné
De son travail muet, profond et acharné.

Mais pour s'épanouir et régner dans sa force,
O les luttes qu'il lui fallut subir, l'hiver!
Glaives du vent à travers son écorce.
Cris d'ouragan, rages de l'air,
Givres pareils à quelque âpre limaille,
Toute la haine et toute la bataille,
Et les grêles de l'Est et les neiges du Nord,
Et le gel morne et blanc dont la dent mord,
Jusqu'à l'aubier, l'ample écheveau des fibres,
Tout lui fut mal qui tord, douleur qui vibre,
Sans que jamais pourtant
Un seul instant
Se ralentît son énergie
A fermement vouloir que sa vie élargie
Fût plus belle, à chaque printemps.

En octobre, quand l'or triomphe en son feuillage,
Mes pas larges encor, quoique lourds et lassés,
Souvent ont dirigé leur long pèlerinage
Vers cet arbre d'automne et de vent traversé.
Comme un géant brasier de feuilles et de flammes,
Il se dressait, superbement, sous le ciel bleu,
Il semblait habité par un million d'âmes
Qui doucement chantaient en son branchage creux.
J'allais vers lui les yeux emplis par la lumière,
Je le touchais, avec mes doigts, avec mes mains,
Je le sentais bouger jusqu'au fond de la terre
D'après un mouvement énorme et surhumain;
Et j'appuyais sur lui ma poitrine brutale,
Avec un tel amour, une telle ferveur,
Que son rythme profond et sa force totale
Passaient en moi et pénétraient jusqu'à mon cœur.

that it drains the pond and surrounding earth
and sometimes it stops, as if astonished
by its silent labour, deep and tenacious.

But to come into blossom and prevail in its strength,
O the struggles that it had to undergo in winter!
Swards of wind across its bark,
howls of the storm, rage of the air,
hoar-frost like rough filings,
all the hatred and all the conflict,
the hail of the East and snows of the North,
the dull white frost whose bite gnaws,
right to the sapwood, the ample skein of fibres,
all the ills that writhe, pain that quivers,
yet never
for a single moment
did its energy diminish
in the steadfast desire that its widening life,
each springtime, should become more lovely.

In October, when gold triumphs in its foliage,
my strides still long, though heavy and wearied,
have often made their long pilgrimage
toward this tree of autumn traversed by winds.
Like a giant brazier of flame and leaf,
it stood aloft, magnificent, under a blue sky,
it seemed inhabited by a thousand souls
that softly sang in its hollow branches.
I went towards it, eyes filled with the light,
I touched it, with my fingers, with my hands,
I felt it stirring deep in the earth
with a movement monumental and superhuman;
and I leant upon it my brute chest,
with such love and such devotion,
that its profound rhythm and all its power
passed into me and penetrated my heart.

Alors, j'étais mêlé à sa belle vie ample;
Je me sentais puissant comme un de ses rameaux;
Il se plantait, dans la splendeur, comme un exemple;
J'aimais plus ardemment le sol, les bois, les eaux,
La plaine immense et nue où les nuages passent;
J'étais armé de fermeté contre le sort,
Mes bras auraient voulu tenir en eux l'espace;
Mes muscles et mes nerfs rendaient léger mon corps
Et je criais: «La force est sainte.
Il faut que l'homme imprime son empreinte
Tranquillement, sur ses desseins hardis:
Elle est celle qui tient les clefs des paradis
Et dont le large poing en fait tourner les portes.»
Et je baisais le tronc noueux, éperdument,
Et quand le soir se détachait du firmament,
Je me perdais, dans la campagne morte,
Marchant droit devant moi, vers n'importe où,
Avec des cris jaillis du fond de mon cœur fou.

PLUS LOIN QUE LES GARES, LE SOIR

L'ombre s'installe, avec brutalité;
Mais les ciseaux de la lumière,
Au long des quais, coupent l'obscurité,
A coups menus, de réverbère en réverbère.

La gare immense et ses vitraux larges et droits
Brillent, comme une châsse, en la nuit sourde,
Tandis que des voiles de suie et d'ombre lourde
Choient sur les murs trapus et les hautains beffrois.

Et le lent défilé des trains funèbres
Commence, avec leurs bruits de gonds

Then, I was as one with that beautiful abundant life;
I felt powerful like one of its branches;
there it stood, an example of the magnificence;
I loved more ardently the soil, the woods, the waters,
the vast bare plain which the clouds pass;
with steadfastness I was armed against fate,
my arms craved to hold within them space;
my muscles and nerves made my body light
and I shouted out: "strength is holy.
Man must leave his mark
peacefully, on his audacious designs:
it is strength that holds the keys of paradise
and whose broad hand pushes open those doors."
And I kissed to distraction the gnarled trunk
and when evening released itself from the firmament,
I lost myself in the dead landscape,
walking straight ahead, no matter where,
with cries gushing from the depths of my mad heart.

FURTHER THAN THE STATIONS, THE EVENING

Shadow takes hold, with brutality;
but scissors of light,
cut through the darkness, with fine strokes
lamp to lamp, along the platforms

The huge station and its wide, straight glass
shine, like a shrine, in the muted night,
whilst veils of soot and heavy shadow
fall on stout walls and high bell towers.

And the slow parade of gloomy trains
begins, with the noise of their hinges

115

Et l'entrechoquement brutal de leurs wagons,
Disparaissant – tels des cercueils – vers les ténèbres.

Des cris! – et quelquefois de tragiques signaux,
Par-dessus les adieux et les gestes des foules.
Puis un départ, puis un arrêt – et le train roule
Et roule avec des bruits de lime et de marteaux.

La campagne sournoise et la forêt sauvage
L'absorbent tour à tour en leur nocturne effroi;
Et c'est le mont énorme et le tunnel étroit
Et la mer tout entière, au bout du long voyage.

A l'aube, apparaissent les bricks légers et clairs,
Avec leur charge d'ambre et de minerai rosé
Et le vol bigarré des pavillons dans l'air
Et les agrès menus où des aras se posent.

Et les focs roux et les poupes couleur safran,
Et les câbles tordus et les quilles barbares,
Et les sabords lustrés de cuivre et de guitran
Et les mâts verts et bleus des îles Baléares,

Et les marins venus on ne sait d'où, là-bas,
Par au delà des mers de faste et de victoire,
Avec leurs chants si doux et leurs gestes si las
Et des dragons sculptés sur leur étrave noire.

Tout le rêve debout comme une armée attend:
Et les longs flots du port, pareils à des guirlandes,
Se déroulent, au long des vieux bateaux, partant
Vers quelle ardente et blanche et divine Finlande.

Et tout s'oublie – et les tunnels et les wagons
Et les gares de suie et de charbon couvertes –
Devant l'appel fiévreux et fou des horizons
Et les portes du monde en plein soleil ouvertes.

and the brutal clash of their carriages
disappearing – like coffins – into the darkness.

Shouts! – and sometimes ill-fated signals,
above the farewells and gestures of the crowd.
Now a departure, now a halt – and the train rolls
and rolls with the clamour of files and hammers.

The guileful country and the savage forest
absorb it turn by turn in their nocturnal fright;
and the giant mountain, the narrow tunnel
and a whole ocean, there at the journey's end.

At dawn, brigs appear, light and clear
with their cargo of amber and rosy ore
and multi-coloured flags fluttering in the breeze
and the delicate rigging where macaws perch.

And the reddish jibs and saffron sterns,
the twisted cables and vicious keels,
portholes waxed with copper and bitumen
and the green and blue masts of the Balearic Isles,

and sailors come from who knows where,
out there, across oceans of splendour and fanfare,
with their songs so soft and gestures so weary
and carved dragons on their black hulls.

The whole dream waits, poised like an army:
and the long waves of the port, like wreathes,
unfurl, alongside ancient vessels, leaving
for Finland, ardent, white and divine.

And all is forgotten – the tunnels and carriages,
the stations covered with soot and coal –
before the wild and febrile summons of horizons
and in full sun the doors of the world stand open.

TEMPS GRIS

La Mer du Nord n'est elle-même
Qu'aux jours rugueux d'hiver,
Quand ses vagues à l'infini sont blêmes
Et ses sables, jusqu'au printemps, déserts.

Toute sa patience avide et sourde
Travaille alors à son énormité
D'embruns compacts, de vagues lourdes
Et de mornes clartés.

Si, vers midi, les cieux noirs se dérident,
L'instant vite s'enfuit, l'instant vermeil
Où se traîne, sur les grèves torpides,
L'or fatigué des vieux soleils.

Et l'ombre, à coups de lumière éventrée,
Se referme, sitôt que l'horizon hagard
Soulève, avec les blocs de sa marée,
Les flux montants de ses brouillards.

Et la mer, boudeuse et vomissant l'écume,
Recommence sa lutte et ses combats,
Engloutissant, derrière un mur de brumes,
Tant de voiles qu'on ne voit pas.

LE PÉRIL

On écoute rouler comme un tonnerre d'eau
Là-bas, au loin, sur la mer grise;
Et les vagues, ainsi que des blocs d'eau
Monumentaux,
Sur le sable se brisent.

GREY WEATHER

The North Sea is only herself
in the rough days of winter,
when the infinite waves are pale
and her sands, until spring, are deserted.

All her hungry, muffled patience,
toils then for her vastness
of dense spray, heavy waves
and mournful brightness.

If towards noon, the cheerless dark skies ease
the moment vanishes, the deep red moment
where, over the torpid beaches
drags the weary gold of aged suns.

And the shadow, from the blows of burst open light
withdraws, as soon as the wild horizon
sweeps up, with the mass of her tides,
the swirling of her fogs.

And the sea, sulky and spewing foam,
begins anew her combats and her trials,
engulfing, behind a wall of mists,
so many unseen sails.

THE DANGER

A thunderous roll of water is heard
in the distance, on the grey ocean, out there;
and the waves, like blocks of water,
monumental,
break apart on the sands.

Les yeux menus des petites lumières
Veillent partout dans les chaumières
Et regardent, depuis hier soir,
La mer gronder sous l'envoûtement noir.

Derrière un mur de brume,
Ils sont partis, les pêcheurs roux;
Ils s'acharnent, mais Dieu sait où,
Parmi des monts de tempête et d'écume.

Avec leur âme, avec leur corps,
Avec leurs yeux brûlés de sel,
Avec leurs doigts mordus de gel,
Ils travaillent contre la mort.

Ils s'appellent et ne s'entendent pas.
L'Ouest, le Nord, toute la mer fait rage;
Le mât
Crie et tremble de haut en bas,
Comme une bête en un naufrage.

Le bateau meurt et se disjoint,
Et se creuse une fosse en la vague profonde;
Et les phares lointains apparaissent plus loin
Que s'ils régnaient an bout du monde.

Et néanmoins les petites lumières
Veillent toujours dans les chaumières;
Et parsèment les enclos noirs,
Comme les miettes du pain d'espoir.

Et les femmes, sous leurs manteaux funèbres,
Le poing crispé contre la bouche,
Sont là toujours, muettes et farouches,
A regarder vers les ténèbres.

The tiny eyes of little lights
in the cottages everywhere keep watch
observing, since yesterday evening
the sea roar under black bewitchment.

Behind a wall of mist,
they set out, the red-haired fisherman;
they battle on, only God knows where
amongst the summits of storm and spray.

With their souls, with their bodies,
with their eyes stung by salt,
with their fingers bitten by frost,
they struggle against death.

They call out and are not heard.
West, North, the whole sea in wrath;
the mast
cries out and quivers from top to bottom,
like a beast in a wrecked vessel.

The boat is doomed and comes apart,
ploughs a pit in the deepest wave;
the far off lighthouses seem farther still
as if reigning at the limits of the world.

Yet nevertheless the tiny lights
still keep watch from the cottages;
scattered amongst the dark enclosures
like crumbs of hope.

And the women, in their mourning capes,
clenched fists to their mouths,
are for ever there, silent and iron-willed,
gazing into the darkness.

MIDI

Et midi luit comme un glaive:
La mer lasse ne peigne plus
Ses flots bouffants et chevelus
Au long des grèves.

Le silence est total et la torpeur
Est si vide qu'elle fait peur.
En vain s'étend le ciel sur le temps et l'espace,
Aucun nuage, aucun oiseau ne passe.

Le soleil chauffe à blanc,
Et seul un peu de sable lent
Sans qu'aucun vent le ride,
Se détache, très doucement,
Du flanc de la dune torride.

LE PORT DÉCHU

Un pauvre phare aveugle, où mord la rouille;
Quelques ancres sur le môle désert,
Un cabestan fendu qui plus ne sert,
Et, tout au loin, le pas d'une patrouille.

Nulle chanson de matelot ne brouille
Les fils du silence tissés dans l'air,
Des gens muets rentrent par nombre pair
En des maisons antiques qu'on verrouille.

Pourtant, au coin du quai, s'élève encor,
Battue et gémissante au vent du Nord,
L'image, en bois sculpté, de la Fortune.

Mais que vienne l'instant où la nuit choit,
L'eau se ternit et plus ne mire en soi,
Jusqu'au matin, que l'or mort de la lune.

NOON

Noon shines like a sword:
The weary sea no longer combs
the billowing hair of waves
along the shore.

The silence is complete and the torpor
is so empty it strikes fear.
In vain the sky extends over time and space,
no cloud, no bird will pass.

The sun heats white
and only a little slow sand
without any wind to wrinkle the surface
detaches itself, so very softly
from the flank of the torrid dune.

THE FALLEN PORT

A poor blind lighthouse, bitten by rust;
a few anchors littering the abandoned pier,
a riven capstan, bereft of purpose,
footfalls of a patrol in the distance.

No sailor's song clouds
the threads of silence woven in air,
the silent drift back, in even number
to ancestral dwellings they firmly lock.

Yet, in a corner of the wharf, still rises
beaten, groaning in the wind of the north,
the image of Lady Fortune sculpted in wood.

But when the moment comes for night to fall,
the water becomes dull and till dawn,
mirrors only the dead gold of the moon.

Dans le bassin aux bords tranquilles,
Les mâts semblent un jeu de quilles
Debout sur l'eau;
La lune est claire et clairs sont les nuages,
Et les voiles et les cordages
Laissent, sur les cargaisons sombres
Des longs bateaux,
Tomber leurs ombres.

Une seule lanterne brille au loin;
Un seul veilleur est le témoin
Du calme entier et du silence;
A peine un menu vent rapide et vain,
Agite-t-il au quai du Rhin,
Le branchage aminci et dépouillé des ormes:
La ville au loin et son port dorment.

Dormez, la ville, et vous, les gens,
Sous le ciel glacial d'un décembre d'argent;
Dormez, les bateaux et les voiles,
Sous les fixes regards d'un million d'étoiles;
Dormez, les âtres froids et les bois consumés,
Et vous, les toits, les murs et les maisons, dormez.

Pourtant, de ci, de là, des clartés brillent;
La face ronde d'un marin
Paraît, soudain,
Au trou carré d'une écoutille.
Les yeux d'un chat luisent furtivement;
Le carillon sursaute et s'exalte un moment,
Et minuit tinte.

Alors,
Le petit port,
Dont la vie est éteinte,
Sous les micas poudreux du givre étincelant,
Semble toute la nuit brûler d'un beau gel blanc.

ALONG THE QUAY

At the basin's peaceful edge
the masts seem like skittles
so erect there on the water;
the moon is clear and clear are the clouds,
the sails and the ropes
cast, on the dark cargo
of long ships,
their shadows.

A lone lantern shines in the distance;
a lone watcher is the witness
of the unbroken calm and silence;
a faint wind swift and shallow
barely stirs the Rhine's quay,
the thinning bare branches of the elms:
the town in the distance and her port sleep on.

Town, sleep on and you, its people,
beneath the glacial sky of a silver December;
sleep on, boats and sails,
beneath the stare of a million stars,
sleep on, cold hearths and burned woods,
and you roofs, walls and houses, sleep on.

Yet, here and there, brightness beams;
the round face of a sailor
suddenly appears
in the square hole of a hatch.
The eyes of a cat furtively gleam;
for a moment the carillon startles and exalts
and midnight chimes.

And so,
the little port,
whose life is lost
beneath the powdery micas of sparkling rime,
seems to burn night long with a sublime white frost.

LE NAVIRE

Nous avancions, tranquillement, sous les étoiles;
La lune oblique errait autour du vaisseau clair,
Et l'étagement blanc des vergues et des voiles
Projetait sa grande ombre au large sur la mer.

La froide pureté de la nuit embrasée
Scintillait dans l'espace et frissonnait sur l'eau;
On voyait circuler la grande Ourse et Persée
Comme en des cirques d'ombre éclatante, là-haut.

Dans le mât d'artimon et le mât de misaine,
De l'arrière à l'avant où se dardaient les feux,
Des ordres, nets et continus comme des chaînes,
Se transmettaient soudain et se nouaient entre eux.

Chaque geste servait à quelque autre plus large
Et lui vouait l'instant de son utile ardeur,
Et la vague portant la carène et sa charge
Leur donnait pour support sa lucide splendeur.

La belle immensité exaltait la gabarre,
Dont l'étrave marquait les flots d'un long chemin.
L'homme qui maintenait à contrevent la barre
Sentait vibrer tout le navire entre ses mains.

Il tanguait sur l'effroi, la mort et les abîmes,
D'accord avec chaque astre et chaque volonté,
Et, maîtrisant ainsi les forces unanimes,
Semblait dompter et s'asservir l'éternité.

THE SHIP

We were advancing, calmly, beneath the stars;
the oblique moon wandered around the bright craft,
and the white terracing of spars and sails
laid upon the ocean its giant shadow.

The cold purity of blazing night
glinted in space and quivered on the water;
you could see The Great Bear and Perseus
high above, as if in a dazzling shadow circus.

On the forward and the mizzen mast,
from stern to bow where lights were darting out,
clear and continuous as chains, commands
suddenly given became linked to one another.

Each gesture served another wider one
and to it devoted the moment of its fruitful ardour,
and the wave carrying the hull and its load
offered them the support of its lucid grandeur.

The sublime immensity exalted the barge,
whose bow marked the waves with a lengthy path.
The man now in conflict with the helm
felt the whole ship shudder between his hands.

He pitched over dread, death and the abysses,
in accord with each star and every volition,
and thus mastering unanimous forces
seemed to subjugate and subdue the infinite.

TENEBRES

La lune, avec son œil vide et glacé, regarde
L'hiver régner immense et blanc sur le sol dur;
La nuit est d'un total et translucide azur;
Le vent, comme un couteau, soudain, passe et poignarde.

Aux horizons, là-bas, les longs chemins de gel
Semblent, toujours plus loin, trouer les étendues;
Et les étoiles d'or jusqu'au Zénith perdues
Parmi l'éther, toujours plus haut, trouer le ciel.

Les villages blottis dans les plaines de Flandre,
Près des fleuves, des bruyères ou des grands bois,
Entre ces deux infinis pâles, tremblent de froid,
Autour des vieux foyers dont ils remuent la cendre.

LES HEURES DU SOIR

VIII

Lorsque ta main confie, un soir des mois torpides,
Au cellier odorant les fruits de ton verger,
Il me semble te voir avec calme ranger
        Nos anciens souvenirs parfumés et sapides.

Et le goût m'en revient tel qu'il passa jadis
Dans l'or et le soleil et le vent – sur mes lèvres;
Et je revis alors mille instants abolis
Et leur joie et leur rire et leurs cris et leurs fièvres.

Le passé ressuscite avec un tel désir
D'être encor le présent et sa vie et sa force,
Que les feux mal éteints brûlent soudain mon torse,
Et que mon cœur exulte au point d'en défaillir.

THE DARKNESS

The moon, with glacial, vacant eye, observes
winter reign vast and white on the hard ground;
night is an azure translucent and complete;
the wind, a knife, comes suddenly, stabs deep.

Yonder, on the horizons, the long tracks of frost
seem ever to pierce the expanses,
and stars of gold as far as the zenith,
amid the ether, ever higher, pierce the sky.

Villages huddled in the plains of Flanders,
near the moor, the rivers, the great forests,
between these two pale infinities shudder with cold
around old hearths, whose ashes they rake.

THE EVENING HOURS

VIII

When your hand confides, on an evening of torpid months,
in the cellar pungent with the fruits of your orchard,
it seems I see you calmly stow away
    our old memories sapid and fragrant.

And the taste returns to me as it once passed
in the gold, in the sun and the wind – across my lips;
and so I see again a thousand obliterated moments
and their joy, their laughter, their cries, their fevers.

The past resurrects with such yearning
to be the present still, its life and strength,
that suddenly the flames, poorly extinguished, burn my body,
and my heart exalts till it almost fails.

O beaux fruits lumineux en ces ombres d'automne,
Joyaux tombés du collier lourd des étés roux,
Splendeurs illuminant nos heures monotones,
Quel ample et rouge éveil vous suscitez en nous.

XXVI

Lorsque tu fermeras mes yeux à la lumière,
Baise-les longuement, car ils t'auront donné
Tout ce qui peut tenir d'amour passionné
Dans le dernier regard de leur ferveur dernière.

Sous l'immobile éclat du funèbre flambeau,
Penche vers leur adieu ton triste et beau visage
Pour que s'imprime et dure en eux la seule image
        Qu'ils garderont dans le tombeau.

Et que je sente, avant que le cercueil se cloue,
Sur le lit pur et blanc se rejoindre nos mains
Et que près de mon front sur les pâles coussins,
Une suprême fois se repose ta joue.

Et qu'après je m'en aille au loin avec mon cœur
Qui te conservera une flamme si forte
Que même à travers la terre compacte et morte
Les autres morts en sentiront l'ardeur!

LES OMBRES

Trouant de tes rayons sans nombre
Le feuillage léger,
Soleil,
Tu promènes, comme un berger,

O beautiful radiant fruits in these autumn shadows,
gems fallen from the heavy necklace of russet summers,
splendours enlightening our monotonous hours,
what ample red awakening in us you arouse.

XXVI

When you close my eyes to the light,
kiss them at length, for they will have given you
all that can be held of passionate love
in their final fervour's final glance.

Beneath the fixed radiance of the sepulchral flame,
lean towards their farewell your sad and lovely face
so that it imprints on them and remains the only image
    they'll guard in the grave.

And that I feel, before the coffin lid is nailed down,
on the pure white bed our hands enjoin
and beside my brow upon the pale cushions,
for a supreme moment your cheek rest.

And that after I slip away with my heart
which will preserve for you a flame of such power
even across an earth compacted and dead
the other dead will sense its ardour!

THE SHADOWS

Piercing with your myriad rays
the light foliage,
sun,
like a shepherd you walk

131

Le tranquille troupeau des ombres
Dans les jardins et les vergers.

Dès les matin, par bandes,
Sitôt que le ciel est vermeil,
Elles s'étendent
Des enclos recueillis et des humbles maisons.
Leur masse lente et mobile
Orne les toits de tuiles
Et les pignons;
Les angélus des petites chapelles
D'une voix grêle les rappellent;
Midi les serre en rond
Autour les troncs.
En petits tas, elles prolongent leur sieste
Jusqu'au moment où s'animent les champs:
L'heure sonnant alors joyeuse et preste
Les disperse sur le penchant
Des talus verts et des collines.
Déjà les brouillards fins tissent leurs mousselines
Fines,
Que l'ombres se ravivent encor
Et s'allongent et s'étalent dans le décor
Et le faste sanglant des fleurs et des fruits rouges,
Pour ne rentrer qu'au soir où plus ni vent ni bruit
Ne bougent,
Toutes ensemble, au bercail de la nuit.

L'ORAGE

Parmi les pommes d'or que frôle un vent léger
Tu m'apparais là-haut, glissant de branche en branche,
Lorsque soudain l'orage accourt en avalanche
Et lacère le front ramu du vieux verger.

the peaceful herd of shadows
through gardens and orchards.

Since morning, in bands,
as soon as the sun is deep red,
they spread
from the gathered plots and humble dwellings.
Their slow and mobile mass
adorns the tiled roofs
and the gables;
the angelus of the little chapels
recalls them with reedy voice;
noon tightens them in circles
around the trunks.
In little heaps, they prolong their siesta
till the moment the fields come to life:
chiming of the hour so joyful and nimble
disperses them over the slope
of hills and verdurous banks.
Already the delicate mists weave their fine
muslin,
but the shadows still revive,
recline and extend in the setting
and the lavish bleeding of flowers and red fruits,
only returning at evening when no wind nor sound
is moving,
all together, to the fold of night.

THE STORM

Amongst apples of gold a light wind caresses;
you appear to me on high, gliding from branch to branch,
when suddenly the storm rushes up in an avalanche
and slashes the brow of the old orchard.

133

Tu fuis craintive et preste et descends de l'échelle
Et t'abrites sous l'appentis dont le mur clair
Devient, livide et blanc aux lueurs de l'éclair
Et dont sonne le toit sous la pluie et la grêle.

Mais voici tout le ciel redevenu vermeil.
Alors, dans l'herbe en fleur qui de nouveau t'accueille,
Tu t'avances et tends, pour qu'il rie au soleil,
Le fruit mouillé que tu cueillis, parmi les feuilles.

LES MORTS

En ces heures de soir où sous la brume épaisse
Le ciel voilé s'efface et lentement s'endort,
Je marche recueilli, mais sans vaine tristesse,
Sur la terre pleine de morts.

Je fais sonner mon pas pour qu'encore ils l'entendent
Et qu'ils songent, en leur sommeil morne et secret,
A ceux dont la ferveur et la force plus grandes
Refont le monde qu'ils ont fait.

Ils ne demandent pas qu'une douleur oisive
Se traîne avec des pleurs autour de leurs cercueils.
Ils comprennent la part que l'œuvre successive
Fait à la joie et à l'orgueil.

Leur esprit est en nous, mais non pas pour nous nuire
Et nous pousser, à contre-jour, comme à tâtons.
Leur voix est douce encor alors qu'on l'entend bruire
Mais que c'est nous, nous qui chantons.

Car l'heure est nôtre enfin; et la belle lumière
Et le sol et les flots et les ronflants essaims

You flee timourous and nimble, descend the ladder
and take shelter under the lean-to whose bright wall
turns white and livid with lightning flashes
and whose roof rings out under rain and hail.

But now the whole sky turns deep red again.
So, in flower-filled grass which welcomes you afresh,
you advance and reach for, laughing now in the sun,
the damp fruit you picked, there, amongst the foliage.

THE DEAD

In these evening hours where beneath heavy mist
the veiled sky fades and gradually sleeps,
pensively I walk, but without vain sadness,
upon this earth crowded with the dead.

I make my steps ring so they'll still hear them
and they'll dream, in their doleful and secret slumber,
of those whose greater strength and fervour
re-shape the world they had once made.

They do not ask that an idle anguish
drags itself weeping around their caskets.
They understand the part successive labour
contributes to happiness and honour.

Their spirit is in us but not to do us harm
nor push us, feeling our way, against the light.
They bestow their voice, so one hears the murmur
but it's us, we who are singing out.

For the hour is ours at last; and the lovely light
and the earth and the waves and the roaring swarms

Des forces qu'on entend vibrer dans la matière
Sont asservis à nos desseins.

Autres sont pour nos coeurs et les dieux et les hommes,
Autres pour nos esprits le pouvoir et ses lois.
Un nouvel infini nous fait ce que nous sommes
Et met sa force en notre foi.

Bondissez donc, désir humain, puissance humaine,
Aussi loin que vous porte ou la lutte ou l'accord.
Que votre amour soit neuf et neuve votre haine
Sur la terre pleine de morts.

QUARTIER SINISTRE
(LONDRES)

Des femelles chauves, la peau
Blette et grise comme une pomme,
S'y promènent en habit d'homme,
Les pieds chaussés de crasse et d'eau.

On boxe, on hurle au fond des caves,
Les seuils barrés, les volets clos;
Et les poings durs cassent les os
Des torses nus et des fronts hâves.

Des fillettes dont l'âge ment
Fixent la passante attardée,
Avec leurs yeux de chair dardée
Par les trous noirs du vêtement.

Le gin chauffe et marine l'ombre
Et donne à l'atmosphère un goût;

of forces you hear vibrate in matter
are enslaved to our designs.

For others are our hearts and gods and men,
for others our spirits, the power and its laws.
A new infinity makes us what we have become
and places its strength in our conviction.

Leap then, human longing, human power,
as far as they carry you, struggle or accord.
May your love be fresh and fresh your hate
upon this earth filled with the dead.

SHADY QUARTER
(LONDON)

Bald females, their skin
grey and overripe as an apple,
stroll there in the attire of men,
feet booted with muck and rain.

They box, shriek into cellars' depths,
at doorways barred, shutters closed;
and hard fists break the bones
of bare chests and gaunt brows.

Young girls whose age lies
fix the lingering passer-by
with eyes of beaming flesh
through the black holes of their dress.

The gin warms and marinades the shadow
lends the atmosphere a special flavour;

Des ivrognes choient dans l'égout
Avec, aux dents, le juron sombre.

Mais les minstrels dansent là-bas, gaîment;
Et sur le fronton d'or d'un vieux théâtre,
Deux globes blancs semblent brûler du plâtre
Et insulter aux feux du firmament.

NOVEMBRE EST CLAIR ET FROID

Novembre est clair et froid et sa belle lumière
Se déplie en splendeur sur le pâle gazon;
Un son de cloche au loin fait parler l'horizon
Et dans mon clos fleurit une rose dernière.

S'il fallait que mon cœur se refroidît d'autant
Pour goûter la beauté de cette heure sereine,
Temps, j'admets ta rigueur et j'excuse ta haine
Qui m'impose l'hiver où régnait mon printemps.

Mon désir est sorti de moi-même et du monde
Comme d'un lumineux et colossal palais,
Mais pour aimer encor le temps calme qu'il fait,
Je me sens comme armé d'une arme plus profonde.

Avec sa grande paix la nature entre en moi,
Elle éprouve mon être à sa force éternelle,
Déjà je m'habitue à m'effacer en elle
Et quand viendra la mort, je serai sans effroi.

Tout est tranquille enfin, et la règle est suivie.
De mes longs désespoirs, il ne me reste rien.
Où donc le vieux tourment, où le regret ancien?
Un soleil apaisé se couche sur ma vie.

drunks drop in the gutter
with a dark curse in clenched teeth.

But minstrels dance there, merrily;
and on an old theatre's gold pediment,
two white globes of plaster seem to burn
causing affront to the blazing firmament.

NOVEMBER IS CLEAR AND COLD

November is clear and cold and her lovely light
unfolds in splendour upon the pale lawn;
sound of a distant bell is the horizon's voice
and in my plot a last rose blooms.

If my heart must grow so cold
to taste the beauty of this serenest hour,
time, I accept your severity and excuse your hate
that imposes winter where my spring has reigned.

My desire has departed from me and the world
as from a palace, radiant and immense,
but to still love the peaceful time it forms
with a deeper armoury, I feel myself armed.

With her great peace nature enters into me,
she makes my being experience her eternal force,
already I'm resigned to fade within her
and when death comes, I'll face it without fear.

All is peace at last, and the rule is kept.
Of my lengthy despairs nothing remains.
Where then the old torment, where the old regret?
Upon my life a calm sun sets.

EMILE VERHAEREN (1855-1916) was the most internationally important and distinguished poet of Belgian nationality at the turn of the twentieth century. His creative output was prolific and not only in poetry; Verhaeren contributed countless articles for diverse publications, published influential essays on art and wrote a number of plays. Verhaeren travelled widely and his name

DATE & PHOTOGRAPHER UNKNOWN

on the billing was enough to fill lecture halls across Europe. His friends and supporters included some of the most celebrated names of the epoch – Rilke, Gide, Mallarmé, Valéry, Zweig... – and in England Verhaeren's importance was acknowledged by the leading critics and writers of the day such as Edmund Gosse and Arthur Symons. At the time of Verhaeren's untimely death in Rouen in November 1916, his influence stretched across the continent of Europe as far as Russia, where Mayakovsky and Blok gratefully received his works.

After his death and the cataclysm of the First World War, Verhaeren's work fell into obscurity, a rash of translations into English in 1916 in the wake of his death dwindling to decades of stasis. Now in France and Belgium, with new editions of his works, Verhaeren's name is undergoing a long overdue re-emergence. This first selection of his poems in English for almost a century provides a starting point for a deep probing of the rich legacy left by one of the genuinely great European poets of the early twentieth century.

WILL STONE, born 1966, is a poet, essayist and literary translator who divides his time between Suffolk and the continent. His first poetry collection *Glaciation* (Salt, 2007), won the international Glen Dimplex Award for poetry in 2008. A second collection *Drawing in Ash*, was published by Salt in May 2011 and his third collection, *The Sleepwalkers*, will be published in 2014. Will's translated works include *To the Si-*

lenced – Selected Poems of Georg Trakl Arc, (2005) and more recently a series of books for Hesperus Press, namely a translation of *Rilke in Paris* by Maurice Betz, and further translations of works by Stefan Zweig and Joseph Roth. Will's current projects include a series of essays constituting a 'psycho geographic' exploration of the cultural landscape and art of Belgium.

Also available in the series
ARC CLASSICS: NEW TRANSLATIONS OF
GREAT POETRY OF THE PAST
Series Editor: Jean Boase-Beier

FRANCO FORTINI
Poems
Translated from the Italian by
Michael Hamburger

MARCELIJUS MARTINAITIS
The Ballads of Kukutis
Translated from the Lithuanian by
Laima Vince

VLADIMIR MAYAKOVSKY
Pro Eto – That's What
Translated from the Russian by
Larisa Gureyeva & George Hyde and introduced by John Wakeman
Complete with 11 photomontages by Alexander Rodchenko,
reproduced in colour.

ED. PETER ORAM
The Page and The Fire
POEMS BY RUSSIAN POETS ON RUSSIAN POETS
Selected, translated from the Russian and introduced by
Peter Oram

SALVATORE QUASIMODO
*The Night Fountain:
Selected Early Poems*
Translated from the Italian by
Marco Sonzogni and Gerald Dawe

GEORG TRAKL
To the Silenced: Selected Poems
Translated from the German and introduced by
Will Stone

RAINER MARIA RILKE
Pure Contradiction: Selected Poems
Translated from the German and introduced by
Ian Crockatt

Further titles of poetry in translation are available in
'Arc Visible Poets', 'Arc Translations', 'Arc Anthologies' and
'New Voices from Europe & Beyond' (anthologies)

www.arcpublications.co.uk